Choose Life

The Tools, Tricks, and Hacks of
Long-Term Family Travellers,
Worldschoolers and Digital Nomads

By Daniel Prince

Dedicated to Clair, Kaitlyn, Sophia, Lauren and Samuel.
Another new chapter awaits us!

Copyright © 2017 Daniel Prince. All rights reserved. No part of this publication may be reproduced, distributed, or transmitted in any form or by any means, including photocopying, recording, or other electronic or mechanical methods, without the prior written permission of the author, except in the case of brief quotations embodied in reviews and certain other non-commercial uses permitted by copyright law.

ISBN: 9781549955785

Table of Contents

Testimonials i
Foreword by Brandon Pearce. iii
Introduction vi

Section One: Taking Life into Your Own Hands

Chapter 1 - Screw This. 1

Chapter 2 - Wait. YOU Read a Self-Help Book? 13

Chapter 3 - You Are Doing What? 29

Section Two: Affording the Travel Lifestyle

Chapter 4 - The Sharing Economy 49

Chapter 5 - Education and World Schooling 78

Chapter 6 - Finances and Accounting 102

Section Three: Family Travel

Chapter 7 - Travelling with Kids 125

Chapter 8 - Shitty Travel Advice 135

Chapter 9 - It's Not All Fun in The Sun You Know! 146

Chapter 10 - Life and Travel Hacks 164

Acknowledgements
Bonus Life Lesson

Testimonials

Hello Dan!

I read the book and now **need** to get my wife to read it, too!

For a long time, I've had this nagging feeling that the expected social construct around me is false, and you are a great data point for that. There is a reality that everyone thinks is sacrosanct and that they must adhere to it. That's what I liked about the book -- your 'stick it to the man' approach -- there is another way!

I love the feeling of everyone saying, "You can't do that!"

Then you saying, "But we have done that!"

I had that when I quit my old career and started my new business, but it's been thirteen years now, after reading this book I think it's time to do it again!" - Luke.

Hello, Mr. Prince!

Thank you for being so gracious and for letting me get a sneak-peek of your book - it was utterly amazing!

I want you to know that your family was one of the factors and families my own family looked into when we were deciding about homeschooling. Long story short, I am now a homeschooling junior and I have to say I love it!!

Your family has really inspired mine in the way you do things and just the brave steps you guys took when making that decision. So, thank you once again!

Yours, Paige

Hi Daniel,

Thank you for the advice and sneak peek of your book. I love it! I am hooked totally. Can't wait to read more.

You had a big impact on me when I heard a podcast and dropped you an email several months back.

We have three more sleeps before we head off on our adventure of travelling, world schooling, house swapping and doing things differently...

So excited.

Thanks for being an inspiration....

Jo and family

Foreword

By Brandon Pearce

If you've ever dreamed of traveling the world with your family, then I highly recommend you read this book.

Dan's courage and determination has led him and his family to learn and experience what most families only fantasize about. And your timing is good, because it's never been easier or more affordable to "see the world". The personal experience Dan has gained, along with those he's interviewed will uncover for you just how possible it is to finally live your travel dreams.

By interesting coincidence, I am writing this foreword from the very house where I first met Dan Prince in person over three years ago. It's the home of mutual friends – the Clark family, whom we both met on our travels. This family has an incredible sense of hospitality that brought our two families together one day in the Southern UK, when we previously had only communicated online.

This shared hospitality is one indicator of the opportunity available to long-term traveling families that Dan discusses in this book. Our family has been traveling for over eight years and has lived in and visited over thirty-seven countries. Right now, we're here in the UK for a couple weeks in between meetings for a documentary project we're involved in, and our upcoming conference, the Family Adventure Summit, which is a live event for families interested in long-term travel, location independence, and more.

Two weeks ago, we were in Scotland. Next week we'll be in Belgium, followed by a month or so in Denmark and Sweden, as we visit families we've come to know along the way. And whilst this is a faster pace than we typically tend to travel, we feel fulfilled by the interactions and deepening friendships we enjoy on the journey.

I believe that long-term travel has the power to transform individuals through the awareness we gain by observing ourselves in different circumstances and encountering new people and ideas in a deep and personal way. It also has the power to transform families by spending extended time together and facing travel-induced challenges together.

But I also believe that travel has the power to transform the world by bringing communities together and breaking down barriers that separate us- whether they be cultural, religious, class-based or otherwise. Travel helps us embrace our shared humanity with all of earth's residents, discovering our similarities, whilst learning to appreciate the differences.

If you don't yet feel ready to set off on your own travel adventure, don't worry. One-by-one, Dan shoots down any excuses you may have for beginning the journey. Whether you feel held back by concerns over finances, education, society, health and safety or logistics, by the time you've finished this book, you'll have the knowledge and motivation to take the next step.

This movement is growing. Over the years, I've interacted with thousands of people who are traveling the world long-term, doing what they're passionate about, and contributing back in their own unique way. In surveys we've performed through the Family Adventure Summit, we've learned just how varied each family's situation is.

For example, some families travel internationally spending under $1,000 per month. Others spend over $10,000 per month. Some families travel from a home base for part of the year. Others are completely nomadic. Some work a regular job, online or off. Others have businesses, freelance gigs or other creative forms of online income. Some put their kids in various types of schools. Others learn without school.

Each family is finding their own way to incorporate travel into their lifestyle. If you are motivated, you will find yours, too.

As I said, it's never been easier to live the life of your dreams. The enabling technology and supportive communities have never been as readily available as they are now. This book will open your eyes to what's possible for you, so you can go get started making your dreams a reality today.

Have fun and maybe we'll see you on the road!

Brandon Pearce
Founder, Family Adventure Summit

Introduction

> "It's almost impossible for a piece of writing to change someone. It's definitely impossible for it to change everyone. So... who is this designed to reach?"
> - Seth Godin

    I know what you're thinking: Is this book for me? This powerful question from Seth is one I took the time to fully digest. In fact, go back and read it again for yourself right now.

    I considered that question long and hard, before, during and after I wrote this book. I pictured you in my mind's eye and wondered about who you are, what you believe and why you are here with my book in your hands, contemplating whether or not it's worth your time to read what I have worked so hard to put into words.

    You're at a point in your life where something simply feels 'off' with your life balance. You may even be contemplating the possibility of escaping your nine-to-five routine (more like eight-to-eight) and taking back the reins to your own life.

    But you don't know where to start.

    You've got responsibilities, including a spouse and kids to care for. You're wrestling with what seem to be two opposing forces: the duty to bring home the bacon and your desire for greater freedom from a soul-sucking job. You want to provide for your family, but you've realised that your current path to achieve that goal has made you nothing more than a weekend lodger in your own home.

    And so you've begun searching for a different path. Maybe you've talked to friends about your frustrations at work, found a blog article or two about family travel, or even joined a forum online to discuss establishing a source of location independent income. But you're still not sure how to put all the pieces of the puzzle together. And now you're here, with my book in your hand, and you're wondering, "Is this book for me?"

Well, let's get to the crux of it right now.

This book is for you, the life-balance-seeker, the nine-to-five escapist, and the family provider who actually wants to spend time with your family instead of working your life away for somebody else.

You just need that social proof, the validation of knowing that somebody else has already taken that huge leap of faith into the unknown before you and kindly trodden a slightly beaten path for you to explore.

Now, take a deep breath and get ready for what you never thought you would find: a book that does just that.

In fact, by picking up this book you are further down the path to your freedom than you ever thought possible. This likely isn't the first stage of your search for a proper escape route. You have already done much of the work over countless conversations about saying goodbye to the nine-to-five life and taking off to travel the world with your family. Your subconscious has already run wild with the endless hurdles, outcomes and possibilities to make it all happen, probably keeping you awake at night and daydreaming in the office!

You've realised what 95% of the population has yet to discover: there could be a different path, another choice. That's a phenomenal first step, but if you're anything like I was, you're probably thinking, "Okay, now what? How do I go from wanting something different to actually achieving it?"

When my wife and I made the big realisation that we needed to change our lives, we didn't have much else to go on to guide us toward that lifestyle. In an effort to make the process a little easier for those who are following in our footsteps, I have written the book that I wish my wife and I had had at our disposal when we were making the biggest decision of our lives.

This book is the final piece of your puzzle.

Come the end of it, you won't be daydreaming anymore. There will be no more time for procrastination. You will clear your head by killing the inner demons and will silence your doubters by knowing the answers to all their "what ifs" and "how-tos" for every step of the journey. Your plans will be put into massive action mode, propelling you and your family headfirst into the life you want to lead!

If that sounds like exactly what you need, then this book is for you.

> "This is your last chance. After this, there is no turning back. You take the blue pill - the story ends, you wake up in your bed and believe whatever you want to believe. You take the red pill - you stay in Wonderland and I show you how deep the rabbit-hole goes."
>
> - Morpheus

From the Well of Experience

Now, if you've read this far, you are most likely starting to wonder, who the hell is Daniel Prince?

In a nutshell, I am a husband and father of four young children who quit his career and what is commonly conceived to be 'life' to travel the world with my young family.

My family's story comes with a personal message for you about how life doesn't have to be what it has randomly shaped out to be. As you read on, I will tell you how we — a family of six — shaped our lives, bent the rules and hacked ourselves into a different way of living. We decided that we wanted to travel the world and so we did, all via the sharing economy.

And, guess what, you can do it, too!

You have the power to change your life, and it is so much easier than you ever thought possible.

If you have a nagging doubt in your mind that life should be better than it currently is, read on. If you want to spend more time with your family, read on. If you want to get off the treadmill, travel and experience a totally different lifestyle, then read on, dear friend!

Throughout our family's journey, we have all flourished in more ways than we could have ever imagined. We have disproved many of our own fears (as well as those of other people) and have especially debunked the fears centred around our kid's education with regards to homeschooling whilst travelling — also known as world schooling.

We have explored temples in Cambodia, watched whales from a private plane in New Zealand, zip lined from the highest peak in Switzerland, privately toured Googleplex in San Francisco, test driven a Tesla, home swapped over sixty times (including a swap with a British rock star) and visited over fifteen different countries across four different continents.

And now I've turned those experiences into the words on these pages, and I guarantee you that they will open up doors you probably never thought could be opened.

With this book in your hands, you now have an invaluable tool at your disposal to achieve a similar experience for your family. If we did it with four young kids in tow, you can do it, too. Don't for one second doubt that.

If the only result of you reading this book is that a seed is planted in your mind that helps you see that there is another way to live your life, I would have already succeeded in my goal.

However, what excites me the most is the thought that some of you might actually take action and leave what you know behind to find another way. If you do, I am convinced that the action you take will affect you, your loved ones and your children (or future children) in the most incredibly positive way.

Nothing is more important than gifting our children the opportunity to view life in an unbiased and experiential manner. Opening brilliant young minds that can carry hope and fresh ideas into the next 100 years is paramount to our world and human existence! By choosing to read and act on the ideas in this book, you can not only change your own life but also pave the path for the generations that will follow you.

Kites rise highest against the wind - not with it.
- Winston Churchill

Just imagine that we're two long-lost friends who ran into each other at the bar and I'm telling you about a different way of living that my family has embraced since we said 'goodbye' to day-to-day life and 'hello' to adventure. We'll certainly have some laughs and you will undoubtedly question my thinking and some of the actions and decision we have made, but you will also walk away from the conversation questioning certain areas of your own life.

The benefit of having this conversation in a book instead of over drinks, however, is that I will be able to supply you with links to TED talks and other tools that inspired us to look at life differently and helped us along the way to homeschool, travel long-term, home swap around the world, leverage the sharing economy, write articles for travel magazines, appear as guests on podcasts, get featured in newspapers, build a blog, write a book and much more.

You can read any chapter in any order. This isn't a novel that has to be read from one chapter to the next. Earmark the book, underline it, follow links, circle paragraphs and quotes, use it, abuse it, and dive into the message head on.

Above all, I hope you have fun reading it and that it helps you in some way. Your life is your legacy. Choose today to make every moment of that life a reflection of your highest aspirations.

Most importantly, enjoy the ride!

Daniel Prince
The Dordogne Region, France 2017

> "Don't go around saying the world owes you a living. The world owes you nothing. It was here first."
>
> - Mark Twain

Chapter 1
Screw This

"We start off with high hopes, then we bottle it. We realise that we're all going to die, without really finding out the big answers. We develop all those long-winded ideas which just interpret the reality of our lives in different ways, without really extending our body of worthwhile knowledge, about the big things, the real things. Basically, we live a short disappointing life; and then we die. We fill up our lives with shite, things like careers and relationships to delude ourselves that it isn't all totally pointless."
- Irvine Welsh, Trainspotting

Deep somewhere in suburbia, a thirty-something male sleeps soundly in his bed, the bedside clock radio glows 5:44 a.m., everything is quiet.

The red devil numbers click to 5:45 a.m. Instantly, music set on low volume from a radio station tugs the man awake. He sits up, immediately alert with a mix of fear and anxiety in his eyes and clicks the radio silent to minimise the disturbance.

He slowly stands and trudges into the bathroom, turns on the shower and steps inside. Wincing at the coldness of the water that rushes over his body, he tenses and gasps for air.

He rushes through the rest of his shower, brushes his teeth and tiptoes back into the bedroom so as not to wake his sleeping wife and young baby.

Silently, he slips into his underwear, shirt and trousers, then fixes his watch. Gently, he kisses his family goodbye as they sleep and walks out of the bedroom, down the stairs, through the front door and into another day of the same old shit as yesterday.

In 2013, I read a book and then promptly resigned from my career. My wife and I gave notice to our landlord, took our four kids out of school, sold almost everything we owned and left a country we had called home and in which we had lived, built a successful career, and raised our family for fifteen years.

But why?

At this stage in our lives, my wife Clair and I were thirty-seven years old and had four children aged seven, five, two and two (yes, we had doubled down on our child quota with a surprise twin pregnancy).

We were a young British family living in Asia. We loved our lives in Singapore, where we had moved as twenty-two-year-old boy and girlfriend to follow my career in the Foreign Exchange Brokerage market.

We worked and socialised alongside people from all over Asia, India, Japan, Hong Kong, China, South Korea and beyond. Everybody had an interesting story to tell about their different business operations all over the world, mixed with many wonderful travel stories and adventures of people overcoming and learning about cultural differences and seeing the most incredible sights.

We built many lifelong friendships with other expats based on the island -- people from Australia, America, Canada, New Zealand and from all over Europe -- and learned from their own cultures, outlooks on life and different businesses.

We were immediately exposed to incredible, new, and fascinating foods to savour and learn to cook. It was an enormous awakening to all of our senses and we quickly embraced the huge learning curve that we found in front of us.

We loved it, every minute of it.

However, like everything, all good things must come to an end. Fast forward fifteen years and times had changed, the country had changed, and my business had changed. Damn it, we had changed. We were fully blinkered and totally trapped on the hamster wheel of a repeated day-to-day, unchallenging, uninspiring and unfulfilling 'life'.

Something wasn't right with our lives and it needed fixing, but shit that was scary!

We knew that it needed fixing long before we finally fixed it, we truly did; but like many people in this same predicament, we just kept kicking the can down the road. We harboured some kind of entitled belief that everything would work out fine if we just carried on grinding it out. We believed that there was some pot of gold waiting at the end of a retirement rainbow for us to cash in on in another twenty to thirty years.

I imagine you might be thinking that way too, but take a minute to stop and consider why we collectively think that way in the first place. The answer is simple: because that is what happened for our parents and grandparents. That is our perceived and socially accepted cycle of life.

Back then, I was of the exact same mindset. It has been hardwired into us, we aren't to blame, it just happened that way. I was ready to work until sixty or seventy years of age and I was damn well counting down the days to when I could retire and put my feet up. I dreamt every day of being old and free.

Sure, I had pipe dreams of escaping young, but how on earth could that be possible? No way pal. I had too much responsibility now and needed to cling onto my rung in the social order -- forget trying to improve it or climb higher. We had the Joneses pushing us all the way. They kept buying bigger houses, newer cars, nicer clothes, the latest phones, joined country clubs and golf clubs, switched their kids' schools, ate out more, took better holidays, the list was endless.

Damn those Joneses!

Making a huge lifestyle change at this stage in life seemed like too much work. It carried too much uncertainty and way too much risk, especially after all the effort we had put into our current lifestyle during the previous twenty years. For many years, I had to push dreams aside, give into the man, listen to my inner fears and voices and resign myself to 'life'.

"Just one more year," I would tell myself. "That's not too hard, just do one more year, then you will be in a better position and a safer place financially to go for it." I can assure you, that 'one more year' is the most depressing year you will ever work.

You will slowly spiral into a pit of angry bitterness each time that inevitable meeting gets called, or that same old customer complaint comes in. The usual let down from a colleague's performance and ever more ridiculous demands from your boss will pile further pressure on top of you.

Come the end of that 'one more year', you will still feel the same way about making a break. But a family dynamic might have changed, or your career might have edged a little further down the gilded path to that next big title on your business card. Thus, the cycle begins again: "Just one more year."

Well, that cycle worked well, too well, and played out just as expected for me, right up until I read that damned book! It finally gave me the push I needed to quit my career, sell everything, and go!

"'Someday' is a disease that will take your dreams to the grave with you."
- Timothy Ferriss - The 4-Hour Workweek

The book's message smacked me in the face. It made everything crystal clear. It bulldozed the forest of doubt and darkness that stood between my family and me and a life we could truly call our own — one we could enjoy to the max and be proud to live. It made me realise that all of that doubt and fear was in my head and the way to overcome it was to face it head on and just go for it.

I was sold. The book had given me the guts to go for it and I was ready for the challenge of whatever came next. The proposition of living our own lives seemed far more exciting and challenging than anything else that lay ahead of us.

But ...

My wife hadn't read the same book, nor had my kids or my extended family, nor had 99.9% of my friends or colleagues.

How was I going to paint this picture for them of quitting my career, leaving a country we loved, saying goodbye to our friends, not having an income, travelling long term, taking the kids out of school and living life on our own terms for a year?

It all summed up to be quite a pitch on paper. Actually, in hindsight, it summed up to be a huge pitch! A pitch that I possibly — okay, definitely — should have worked on a little longer, finessing the finer details into ... a PowerPoint presentation, maybe?

Some financial graphs might have been a nice addition and, to be fair, perhaps even expected. At the very least, I should have made a detailed timeline with action points and deadlines to meet. Including some solid research that carried a little more weight than a dog-eared copy of a 'self-help book'.

However, always keen to get straight to the point, I shunned the aforementioned pitch ideas, it seemed too time consuming!

Instead, I returned home late one night, after another laboriously boring day and dreadful client dinner, ready and psyched up to have 'the conversation' with my wife about how I believed we should change our lives forever.

I walked through the front door and kicked off my shoes. "Seriously babe, screw this."

"Eh?"

I pressed on.... "This is bullshit, we just aren't living life! What's the point of us having four kids if I don't ever get to see them and you tire yourself out running around after them all day long? I get home, peck the kids on the head as they go up to bed and then flop on the sofa next to you to watch mindless TV."

"Yes, I know," Clair admitted. "I want to make a change, too. I have been trying to think of a way to do this for some time. I am not at all happy with the kids' schooling. It's too suffocating, too black and white, there is no lateral thinking at all. They are just being taught to tick boxes, it's awful, and there is no creativity, play or fun. But what can we do? We seem to be stuck. And each time I try to rationalise this in my head or talk to you about it, you just shut me down and say, 'That's life'."

That was not the answer I was expecting.

Then it sunk in that I had been the one anchoring us into a life of rinse and repeat. I was the one who had blindly accepted the social norm for me to 'have a career'. I felt that I needed to be in the office, providing as best as I could for my family. I had closed my eyes to the fact that the family was suffering because I couldn't face to listen to the complaints of their daily lives. I felt that if I had to be working my ass off all day, then everybody should just be thankful and not be coming to me with problems or complaints.

"I'm starting with the man in the mirror, I'm asking him to change his ways"
- Michael Jackson

But it was true. 100% true. I had been the guy pushing all of the problems aside and rationalising these issues away with the easy and cowardly way out of shrugging my shoulders and saying 'That's Life'.

But wasn't the situation we found ourselves in actually the complete opposite of life?

Think about it. "That's life." Let that sink in for a second. Three words. THAT IS LIFE.

LIFE.

How is it that somehow, we all end up painting ourselves into this shitty corner of get up, go to work, deal with ungrateful customers, psychopath colleagues, unrealistic goals, meetings, phone calls, KPIs, budgets, pay cuts, humiliation, elation and deflation?

And for what? A pay cheque. That is it. A pay cheque we spend on useless crap that makes us feel better for an instant, but realistically buys us nothing.

Really?

What I had read had awakened a giant. It lit a burning desire within me to prove to myself (and, seemingly, the world at large) that I could live my life on my terms. I could spend every minute of the day with my family by my side, if not forever, for at least one year.

It was time for us to be selfish with our own lives. Our story – this book you are now reading – is proof that we did it. We pulled it off. In fact, we absolutely nailed it and travelled non-stop around the world for two and half years via the sharing economy.

At the time of writing, we are renting a house in The Dordogne region of France for nine months so that we can immerse ourselves in the culture and learn the language.

Why? Because that's what we want to do. That's why.

But don't think for one second we found it easy. We had demons to face and barriers to cross. I will share them with you in the pages ahead so you can learn from our experience. We had many doubters to contend with; we were, after all, going against the grain of social acceptance and the general order of things.

Before we jump in deeper, however, let me share a personal journal entry from the hectic and anxious days when we were making the biggest decision of our lives. It will give you a small glimpse into the mindset that finally pushed us out the door and into the life of our dreams.

I remember clearly where I was when I wrote this entry. It was the first day back in the office after a five-day family break over the New Year's holiday. I was miserable, I didn't want to be there and the thought of another year of the same old crap was digging into me.

I switched on the PC, opened my online journal and started thrashing at the keys. I needed to get my thoughts out and onto paper. I needed to vent and it was great therapy. Once I read it back to myself, I knew my mindset had changed forever, and so would my life.

Online Journal - Jan 6th, 2014

It is not the fear of the unknown we should be afraid of.

No, it is the fear of repeating the same day-to-day rituals of blinkered, expected and guided life that should truly terrify us all.

Take action, nobody will hand you the life you want, nobody will say ...

'Hey Dan, go watch a movie with your kids on your lap, go travel with the family, go play in the swimming pool, spend real, REAL time with your wife, not time dictated by calendars and commitments.'

You need to bend the rules yourself, just slightly. Don't fear change, fear the norm!

How terrifying is waking up every morning to an alarm clock to drag yourself into a repeat of the day before, a total Groundhog Day, the same meetings, talking to the same customers, dealing with the same crap for the next twenty years and missing your kids grow up? That dread is what is truly terrifying, not change!

Think about that first day "back to life" after a holiday. It's so depressing. Stay strong, stay focused, take a deep breath and step off the treadmill.

Stepping off the treadmill was the hardest part of our whole journey, but I'm so glad that we took the leap. Freedom and adventure are on the other side, my friend. I know it's scary, but you've got my story as evidence that it's possible.

"Happiness is not something readymade. It comes from your own actions."
- Dalai Lama

As you read on, it will become clearer how we had to think deeply about our actions and their consequences at each point. I hope the answers we found will help you gain a clearer perspective.

Enjoy the read, for this book is the courage and the validation for which you seek.

Thoughts From Clair

To give you an ampler perspective of what choosing this life was and is truly like, my wife Clair has added some of her own thoughts to each chapter. This will give you a greater understanding and insight into what we were going through at the time, and how we overcame such situations.

Enter Clair –

In general, I loved my life. I had a caring and loving husband who worked hard to keep our life comfortable. I had four beautiful children that, whilst required hard work, kept me happy and put a smile on my face daily. I had many great friends that I had made in the fifteen years that I had lived in Singapore; and I also loved my surroundings.

Singapore was a great place to live and bring up children. I loved the diverse culture that my family was exposed to, I loved the safety and that most things were accessible and relatively easy. The only thing that nagged at me constantly was the schooling that my children were receiving. It drove me crazy with its highly stressful, old-fashioned, black and white ways of feeding information to children.

Due to the sudden arrival of the twins, our whole life changed and we made the decision to move away from private schooling into the public school system. It was very different from the education that I had envisaged for my children. It was strict, blinkered, rote-based learning. The teachers fed information to bored children that sat in rows, the classrooms didn't have pictures on the walls and it was a very black and white, test-based, and high-pressure environment.

Then Dan started reading "the book" and I heard him say things that I had never heard him say before.

I spent all day with the kids, but I wasn't doing fun things. I was waking up sleepy twins from their naps to do school pickups and walk home with sweaty little girls in thirty-seven-degree heat. Then I was rushing to get the kids out of the pool from swimming lessons, get them into their ballet tights (have you ever tried getting a wet child into ballet tights?), before bombing down the highway to get them to their class, whilst thinking that I should be cooking dinner if I want to get the kids into bed at a reasonable time.

I'm not complaining – this is not an unusual family routine. Many people do this and worse, in much worse circumstances! This was my life and I didn't even think about changing it and believed that as the kids got older, it would get easier. Wouldn't it?

However, as Dan started talking to me more and more about his new ideas and of what he was learning, I started thinking, too. I didn't read the book, to be honest. I didn't have time and I probably didn't need to. Dan was paraphrasing all that I needed to know and wouldn't stop talking about it!

But I did start thinking more deeply about our life. I wasn't having fun anymore. I started questioning what this life was all about.

I have always been of the view that if you don't change something, then you can't complain about it. Plus, we were dipping into savings. Surely, if we were spending our savings to live, then we should be doing something more fun, perhaps even reckless!

— — — — — — — — — — — —

TOOLS AND TRICKS

A great tool for defining your future path is to write down where you envisage yourself being in the future. Whether it is in one year, three years or ten years, it doesn't matter. Write it down, envisage where you will be, what your house, car, yacht, or whatever it is you want looks like, who you have met, where you have travelled, the things you have achieved and the lives you have touched. Make it as fantastical as you like, it really doesn't matter, nobody will read it but you. Go for it. Make it as detailed as you can, then simply sit back and see what happens. It's unreal. Believe me, it has worked for me countless times already!

www.Princesoffthegrid.weebly.com is our family website and travel blog, which has followed our journey every step of the way. Feel free to visit the site anytime to connect and say hi.

Huge shout out to **www.weebly.com** who makes it so easy for first timers to build their own websites. I can highly recommend their service, and believe me, I came from zero knowledge of building a website!
This blog post from Mark Manson is, in my opinion, the best thing ever posted on the interwebs, or probably the best thing ever written in the history of ever. It will help you get your mindset into the swing of things! **https://markmanson.net/not-giving-a-fuck**

Mike Lewis is an inspiration to many looking to make the jump! He made the jump himself and has an incredible story to tell. I hope to work closely with Mike over the next few years as he has invited me to work as an ambassador for his programme.

I wish Mike well with his own book, which is to be released in January 2018 through a large publishing company in the U.S. He will even have the foreword written by Sheryl Sandberg. This highlights the work that we are doing is clearly making waves and changing people's lives. Hopefully, together we will be able to reach a much wider audience!

Find Mike and his team at **www.whentojump.com** where you can learn about many more individuals and families who have taken life into their own hands as well.

Andrew Henderson is the creator of **www.nomadcapitalist.com,** where he explains that his "'mission is to show you that geography is no longer a limiting factor and that you can exponentially improve your living situation."

Andrew's blog provides a wealth of information on living, doing business and investing abroad. He also has a fantastic podcast on the same subjects. Look for my interview there as well! Andrew is also hard at work writing and getting ready to release a book of his own soon, so make sure to look out for that!

Lastly, watch Groundhog's Day again, or for the first time if you have never seen it! Not only is it the legendary Bill Murray at his absolute best but the message is clear and funny at the same time! Trust me, it will take on a whole new light after reading this book.

Find the best clips here:
https://www.youtube.com/watch?v=9hq5jZrFTbE

Chapter 2
Wait. YOU Read a Self-Help Book?

"Inaction breeds doubt and fear. Action breeds confidence and courage. If you want to conquer fear, do not sit home and think about it. Go out and get busy."
- Dale Carnegie

My taste buds were tingling. The chicken cashew nut was perfectly spiced, the baby kai lan had just the right amount of garlic-to-oyster sauce ratio and the Tiger beer was blizzard cold.

I sat on my plastic chair at a plastic table enjoying a meal served on plastic plates with plastic chopsticks. I was with a close friend in a Singapore hawker centre, just behind the bustling end of Boat Quay in the CBD. The food was delicious, but most of all cheap!

We had been talking about the usual crap, football, his latest girlfriend(s), business, weather ... you get the picture. He knew I had read 'The Book'. I had been waxing lyrical about it at a past drinks meeting, but he didn't know how much of an impact it had really had on me.

I tried to pick my moment. When and how could I drop the bombshell? I needed to get it off my chest. I wanted some kind of positive reaction but kind of feared the worst.

I dipped a chicken morsel in some chili padi (an insanely hot dipping sauce made from Bird's eye chilies, garlic and soy sauce), shoved it in my mouth and went for it.

"So yeah, I'm gonna quit, (pause ... munch munch). We are going to leave Singapore to travel the world!"

"What on Earth are you talking about? Are you demented?" my mate asked incredulously. "Don't pin your hopes and dreams on the written words of some self-styled self-help guru you idiot! You have a family to think about! You have a career to build and a responsibility to your company."

Bugger.

What a journey since that moment! Who in their right mind would actually believe that reading a 'self-help' book can actually change your life so dramatically, forever?

I was probably the hardest sell of the bunch. I never ever read such books and honestly, I judged people that did. I couldn't figure out why people would read self-help books and then still be in their same job, same position, same state of mind and same rut years afterwards. I would listen to their giddy highs of enlightenment for a couple of weeks, quietly shaking my head in the knowledge that it would all wear off after a week or two and everything would be back to normal.

Which of course, it always was.

So, how did I ever come to read a self-help book? I have a conversation with a different friend to thank for that.

The Book

> "I trust that everything happens for a reason, even if we are not wise enough to see it."
> - Oprah Winfrey

The voice at the end of the line abruptly cut off, leaving me mid-sentence. I swiftly slammed down the phone in a rage of frustration, disbelief and anger. A deal had just gone sour that I had been working on all morning and I was seething.

"What a waste of fucking time! Seriously, what's the point of this shit, why the hell would he do that deal away from me? I set the whole thing up. It was even my idea in the first place. He would never have even thought of it!"

I pushed myself away from my desk, wheeling backwards in my chair, stood and grabbed my mobile phone in the same motion and made a call to a friend as I walked into the empty board room.

"Hey, this morning has been frigging awful, I need some sense in my life. Let's get some lunch today. How about that Ramen place you mentioned last time we met up?"

With the lunch meeting set, I counted down the remaining hours and was out the door on the first chime of the bell.

Walking through the searing heat and 100% humidity of Singapore in the midday sun is no mean feat, and by the time I reached the restaurant I was even more het up and ready to unleash my burdens on a friendly ear.

Instead of enjoying a nice social get-together with a guy I really respected and wanted to have fun with, I spent the entire meeting bitching and moaning about my job and how there had to be another way to live and enjoy life. He listened like a good friend does, whilst probably making a mental note to start avoiding me.

The dreaded time of returning back to the office approached us … and then it happened.

As we got up to leave the table he nonchalantly said, **"You should read *The 4-Hour Workweek* by Tim Ferriss."**

That was it? The great all-conquering advice? I had just outlined how rubbish my life had become and he recommends a self-help book! How many self-help books have you been recommended and just completely ignored?

We shook hands, loosely scheduled a drink for one night in the future and parted ways, walking off into the humidity and ultimate looming misery of the office.

I got back, covered in sweat and headed to my desk situated in a room which lacked natural sunlight. I sat in my chair, which had a broken arm rest, and stared at my PC trying unsuccessfully to avoid listening to the drivel my colleagues were openly discussing. I shrugged and shook my head at how pointless their chatter was and remained shocked by their lack of understanding and urgency with completing or even contributing to their actual workday.

Balls to this. I opened a web browser, searched for the nearest bookstore, called them up and reserved the book. The afternoon dragged laboriously by, and at 5 p.m. I received the gut wrenchingly terrifying news that I had another pointless meeting to attend at 6 p.m.

"Meetings are an addictive, highly self-indulgent activity that corporations and other large organizations habitually engage in only because they cannot actually masturbate."
- Dave Barry

Finally released from my prison at 7 p.m., I dodged the invite of a drink from a colleague and sprinted to the book shop before they closed.

I read the first chapter on the train journey home. Immediately, a light switched on in my mind.

I texted my friend, "Mate, I think you might have just changed my life forever."

I was hooked.

Like an addict, I would find excuses to be alone to read the book, voraciously turning pages and trying to figure out how I could make any of these practices work in my own life. As a thirty-seven-year-old married man with four kids all under eight years of age, I had responsibilities. I had to bring home the bacon. I had to be out the door and into the office every day. I had to entertain clients and be home late two or three nights per week, and I had to be away on business trips some weekends.

That's just what you do, right?

That's the man's role in life, isn't it? We work and work and work, to the point where we become nothing but a glorified lodger in our own homes. Put up and shut up, pay your respect, pay the man and grind through it.

As I completed my first read (there would be five in total) I closed the book and sat dazed, confused, suspicious, convinced yet unconvinced, but above all, excited. What the in the world had I just read?

What a whirlwind of information, suggestions, advice, truths and, for lack of a better word, sense. It all made perfect sense! I turned the book over, re-opened it and started reading from page one again.

That was November 2013. By March 2014, I had quit my job and we had given notice to our landlord, sold almost everything we owned, taken the kids out of school and were leaving a country in which we had lived, built a successful career, called home and raised our family for fifteen years.

All on the back of a book?!

Most friends and family were supportive, some needed time to understand the decision but respected it, and a few thought we were just plain nuts.

But our plan was clear: leave the rat race and travel anywhere we could, just go and be together.

One line from the book resonated throughout my mind the first time I ever read it, and it still does to this day.

> "**Enough is enough. Lemmings no more ... the blind quest for cash is a fool's errand.**"
> - Tim Ferriss

The burning question on your mind right now is likely, "But how can you just decide that enough is enough and suddenly up and leave?"

Ah, if it had only been that simple.

Finding Validation

You see, this was not a decision we took lightly. How could it be? Sure, the book was the catalyst, but my goodness did we go through some soul searching over the next weeks and months before we actually decided, definitively, that we were going to actually go for it.

There is so much to consider when making life changing decisions, whether it be your choice of school, university, career, where to live, getting married, buying a house, having children, the list goes on.

I am sure that there are some books out there that will tell you that there is a correct procedure or process to follow. Well, there isn't. Not one that can magically cover every individual's personal circumstance at that exact moment in their lives. How can there be?

Instead, what one has to do is juggle advice — solicited or unsolicited — and try to figure out the best course of action for them and their family alone.

One thing you should absolutely do when making big decisions, however, is seek validation.

We got clear in our minds that what we wanted to do more than anything was to travel as far and for as long as we could. We agreed that the experience would bring our family together as a unit and open us all up to a learning experience that very few get to enjoy. With this clear goal set, we started researching and looking for people who had done the same.

Were there families out there that were homeschooling their children as they travelled long term? How had it affected their children and family life? Where had they been? How long had they travelled? What pushed them to go?

Amazingly, we found that there is a whole community out there of people that were doing just this!

Some are professional Bloggers, Vloggers, or Digital Nomads who can work independently from anywhere in the world via a laptop. Others just took a life break, a sabbatical or quit their jobs entirely to figure something else out along the way.

> "Nobody ever figures out what life is all about, and it doesn't matter. Explore the world. Nearly everything is really interesting if you go into it deeply enough."
> - Richard Feynman

We found the Pearce Family (at www.pearceonearth.com) via Tim Ferriss's blog. Brandon Pearce had been invited to write a post about running his business remotely whilst travelling long term with his young family. I immediately emailed him with a list of questions, begging to pick his brain. I was desperate, I wanted to believe it was real, I needed validation. Below is the original email I sent to him:

Hey Brandon.

Brace yourself, because this could be a long one, but on the upside, this is a totally personal letter, I am NOT seeking any endorsements or publicity, so I have that going for me! Right?

Anyway, if you do find yourself reading the full letter and are willing to get in contact that's great, if not I totally understand, so here goes.

Six weeks ago, I bought The '4-Hour Work Week *by Tim Ferriss and am already on my third read, I literally get to the last page and turn straight back to page one. This book has finally given me the nudge I needed to throw all of the common wisdom of life out of the window and given me the confidence to take charge of my own destiny, and you sir are the closest thing to living proof as possible; with regards to my own situation, that is.*

Following Tim's blog, I came to learn about your own leap of faith into the great unknown and after reading about you and your journey so far I felt compelled to write you this note.

Let me explain myself further, I am a married male aged thirty-seven with four young wonderful children aged eight, six and three-year-old twins, who I miss immensely all day long whilst I am at work. My wife and I are both British and have lived in Singapore for the last fifteen years where we have grown our family and a wonderful circle of friends.

My career was mainly made up of seventeen years as a Foreign Exchange broker but am currently now in the commodity markets trying to make ends meet. After reading Tim's book and your own story we have now decided to follow as best we can the theories and practices in the book and see if we can make things work for ourselves and truly come together as a family.

Our lease here runs out in ten weeks, so that is our timeline and we are busy now with all of the uncomfortable tasks such as selling 'stuff' and getting admin etc. etc. all in order. How many people do you think have stumbled at this first hurdle?

What a gargantuan task it seems to be, we have SO much furniture and toys and general rubbish that it just seems so much easier at this point to just turn your brain back onto the autopilot deferred life mode and get back on the treadmill of life.

ANY words of wisdom or encouragement about your experience regarding this early stage would be very much appreciated!

Creating a muse (sideline business to earn a small income as per The 4-Hour Work Week) will naturally be a huge part of the operation, or snagging a remote working arrangement for the New Year, but if either of those do not fall into place come March, we will still go. I have one muse already, as a children's book author, so will be able to use time to promote that.

We own a house in Koh Samui, so that will be our first port of call. All I would need is enough money to get food on our table and pay some electric bills and health/travel insurance etc., I can lean into savings for that.

If you are still reading, you are probably thinking 'Hey that's great Dan, random weird dude from the internet, nice story pal, but what does this have to do with me?'

Fear dear Brandon …. FEAR!

When I rationalise all of this in my mind, I KNOW it is what I want, what we should do. BUT, oh my word, the fear is always there, that nagging horrible self-doubt, the close friends or family that tell you that you're mad, that tell you not to 'throw' away everything you have worked for, 'just a few more years, get that little extra bit of money in the bank account' or 'you can't just take the kids out of school'.

I feel the pressure and burden of it all weigh so heavy, and feel that I might really be just trapped in a pipe dream 'following the written words of a self-promoting snake oil salesman' or 'a terrible LAZY father dreaming of early retirement and leading my family into certain disaster'.

This, my dear Brandon, is where you might be able to help, any advice or comparisons from your own experience will certainly give us more strength and help us through to the promised land of REAL life!

> *In truth, you have already helped and I do understand that. The blog is brilliantly written, open and truthful and addresses our biggest fear of education for our kids.*
>
> *So, I will sign off now and leave you to enjoy your day, thank you for taking the time to write this blog, I hope letters such as these validate the time and effort that you put into it.*
>
> *Good luck renovating your house in Bali, what a wonderful place to live, we have been there many times and will return again soon, our favourite spot was dining on the deck at Gado in Seminyak, eating great food and watching the waves roll in.*
>
> *Peace*
>
> *Daniel Prince*

Brandon came straight back to me with a ton of information and friendly practical advice. We have since become good friends and met with the Pearce family as our travels crossed paths, coincidentally on the southern coast of England. Here is Brandon's response:

> *Great to meet you, Daniel, and I empathize with where you're at. It was a big headache getting rid of all our stuff, too. But OH! So liberating once we did. We gave a lot of it away in the end just because we didn't want the hassle of trying to find buyers.*
>
> *Many family and friends didn't understand, but some were supportive, and we've met so many more friends along the way who are. Our relationships with many back home have changed. Especially since we left the Mormon Church, some people (including family) have completely dropped out of our lives. Now we focus on fostering relationships based on authenticity and connection rather than superficial similarities, even if they are genetic.*
>
> *We feel much healthier and alive now. You may want to check out the Families on the Move Facebook group if you want to*

meet more travelling families who've done similar things, and are funding their lifestyles in a variety of ways. There are several hundred families in the group, all over the world.

Fear can always come up. But it's okay. It's just an emotion, usually temporary, and when I see it like that, I find it doesn't have as much ability to control me.

It's usually also not based very much in reality, but often gets carried away into stories that will probably never come true. If they do come true, I'll deal with it at that time. No sense worrying about it now, especially if it's something I have little control over.

I can't promise what your life will be like by making this jump. It's quite a leap of faith to do it without a steady muse first. But people have done the same without even any savings and have made it work. You seem like you have the skills to earn an income wherever you are, perhaps even if it's just getting back into forex. :)

But if you're determined, I don't doubt you'll be fine wherever you go. If you really hate the lifestyle and want to come back, I'm sure you can do that, too, and will have a fresh perspective to guide you into making it even better than before.

Good luck!

Brandon

"Train yourself to let go of everything you fear to lose."
- Yoda

Boom! Validation found and suddenly Brandon was my Yoda! I was stunned to receive such a gracious and lengthy response and immediately shared it with my wife. It was the extra nudge we needed, that little confidence booster.

In his email, Brandon suggested that we become part of the Families On The Move Facebook community. It blew my mind that there was a whole Facebook group for us to join.

In an instant, we now had a connection to over 250 families, all doing what we thought was impossible and all eager to help us in any way at all.

We were offered all kinds of great advice from people who had made the change themselves and were living the life we wanted. They had real, practical, in-the-field advice -- and not a raised eyebrow, tut, or scoff in sight! We were offered places to stay if we needed, invited to meet-ups or put in touch with friends of friends who might be able to aid our travels in any way shape or form.

The human spirit really started to show through and this was just our research phase!

Fear Setting

But there it loomed, that awful, all-crippling emotion of fear telling me to stop being so ridiculous. How could I rationalise this to myself in a clear manner that smashed any of our doubts? In his book, Ferriss outlines a practice he coined as "fear setting". He has even presented a TED talk on the subject. After following his steps of defining our biggest fears, listing the steps we would take if they were ever to actually happen and the probable outcomes, things started to look a lot easier.

There is much more on the subject of fear throughout the book, which I hope will carry you through the doubts you will certainly face, but for now let me give you a quick example of where my head was at when I went through this process.

Dan
Fear: Going bankrupt and never being able to get another job, losing the respect of everyone closest to me and being regarded as a total loser.

Steps needed to take if this actually happened: Move the family into my parents' house where we will be safe, comfortable, loved and fed. Leverage my network, find out who is hiring, get introductions and make approaches.

Probable Outcomes and Benefits: Have a great time

travelling whilst it lasted. Expose the kids to some unforgettable life lessons, cultures, sights and time together, which will be instrumental in defining their personalities, ethics and create forever treasured memories.

Moving in to live with my parents would result in giving them and the grandchildren more time to connect to each other on a new level and would open up the opportunity for us to reconnect with extended family.

Engaging with and leveraging my network would mean reconnecting with old friends, colleagues, customers and getting to meet super interesting new people. It would lead me along a path of self-discovery, opening my eyes to new roles in markets I had never thought about exploring when blinkered with my old career.

Result ...

Dan 1 - Fear 0

I then added another layer of fear setting on top of this and did what is called in the financial markets a Risk/Reward analysis. It's another simple exercise and one you can also apply.

List your biggest risk and then write out the possible rewards. Then you can make a call on whether or not it's worth taking the risk. How high are the stakes on the risk side? If they are too high, don't take the risk. If the rewards far outweigh the risk, then it's worth taking. An example:

Risk: Leaving my Career and losing all the money I had saved.

Reward: Time with my wife and children travelling the world, no boss, no constraints, no career pressures, no business trips, no client b/s, no office politics, the ability to do what I want, when I want.

Result ...

Dan 2 - Fear 0

I remember one final moment of clarity that really helped us see through the dark forest of doubt as we faced this huge moment in our family's lives. Thankfully, I wrote it all down in the journal I kept at the time and can subsequently share it with you, too:

> *Just imagine the feel of dread and regret if in fifteen years from now, when the kids are grown up and gone, we look back at this pivotal point in our lives and we had succumbed to our fears and decided not to go through with it.*
>
> *Think about all the thought and effort we have put into making this decision over the last few weeks. We have ultimately come to the conclusion and knowledge that it is totally achievable. To not action this now would forever leave us asking the question, 'what if?'*
>
> *It really doesn't matter what happens, good or bad it will always be better than not knowing."*

"To travel is to live."
- Hans Christian Anderson

"For the past 33 years, I have looked in the mirror every morning and asked myself: 'If today were the last day of my life, would I want to do what I am about to do today?' And whenever the answer has been 'No' for too many days in a row, I know I need to change something."
- Steve Jobs

TOOLS AND TRICKS

The 4-Hour Workweek by Tim Ferriss has been translated into over thirty languages and spent more than four years on the New York Times Bestseller List.

Tim also hosts a hugely popular Podcast titled the Tim Ferriss

Show. His blog www.thefourhourworkweek.com is where you can find all of his articles and podcast guests.

Tim's TED talk on fear setting:
https://www.ted.com/talks/tim_ferriss_why_you_should_defi ne_your_fears_instead_of_your_goals

> "He's not the messiah, he's a very naughty boy!"
> - Mandy Cohen

Now, as much as I have laid praise to the workings of Tim and his amazing book, there are many other people you can connect with when looking for your own validation!

www.pearceonearth.com is the family blog of the Pearce family, who have been travelling full time for over seven years. They are hugely respected within this niche group of people and are a driving force and voice of the family travel movement. Brandon and Jen are always willing to share their story and love to inspire others.

Brandon has launched a brand-new service called Family Travel Accelerator where he will conduct monthly training programmes. You can learn more at http://brandonpearce.com/p/family-travel-accelerator

Brandon and Jen also founded and run the Family Adventure Summit where you can learn much more about extended family travel from people who have actually done or are doing it.
https://familyadventuresummit.com

Here is the link to Brandon's blog article
https://tim.blog/2013/02/01/case-study-what-does-a-real-4-hour-workweek-look-like-with-a-family/
@Brandags is his twitter handle. Reach out and say hi!

Jason Jenkins is a travelling father and family man who, as I am writing this, is enjoying life in Spain. Jason has a TON of validation resources. His website has links to over eighty podcast episodes that he has conducted with families travelling long-term with children. He covers subjects such as travelling with babies (in fact, many families have fallen pregnant and given birth on the road!), home swapping, house sitting, pet sitting, RV road tripping, sailing around continents together and much, much more. I have personally been interviewed by Jason twice and hope you seek out my voice on his site. ;) www.anepiceducation.com

The Families On The Move Facebook group is an unbelievable source of information and a brilliant group of likeminded people only too happy to reach out and help you. Find the group and reach out to the admin staff, outline your plans, thoughts, desires and short family description and why you would like to join the group. To join this group, you must be a family that travels or that is looking to start travelling soon.

The Worldschoolers Facebook group is also a group of travelling, world schooling or homeschooling families. This group is much bigger in size and perhaps a little more U.S.-based than Families on the Move. You will find a huge amount of information and help here too. This group isn't just about travelling families, it is a highly varied group of people. Some people homeschool, some travel full- or part-time, some are teachers, and some people don't travel but live and educate their children in another country, for example.

The Location Independent Families Facebook group is another place to find help and validation, it is run by Paul Kortman. Paul also has a travel podcast and website at http://homealongtheway.com/

I Am A Triangle is a web page / group aimed at families who have left their country of birth and are fitting in around the world. http://iamatriangle.com/

Fellow traveller Liz Quain has put together an ultimate list of Family Travel Bloggers on her Pinterest account and was only too happy to share it with me here. This is an amazing list of people that you can connect with, thank you Liz!
https://www.pinterest.co.uk/elizabethnyc06/travel-bloggers-

families/ Be sure to check out this list. Look for and learn about the families who have situations closer to your own, then reach out to say hi and find your own mentors!

Http://www.incredibledash.com Describe themselves as "A family of five, travelling fulltime in our RV and embracing each day as a chance to live purposely. We don't know what the future holds but we know we want to live more intentionally, more adventurously and more simply."

Chapter 3
You Are Doing What?

> "Travel is fatal to prejudice, bigotry, and narrow-mindedness, and many of our people need it sorely on these accounts. Broad, wholesome, charitable views of men and things cannot be acquired by vegetating in one little corner of the earth all one's lifetime."
> - Mark Twain

We walked into the restaurant and sat down, ready for a nice, child-free meal.

We were on the island of Phuket in Thailand, taking our yearly family vacation with my parents. The kids were passed out, tired from a whole day in the pool. Our babysitter had arrived dead on time. Everything had gone smoothly and the four of us we were ready for a lovely, stress free Thai meal.

However, things did not go to plan. Not at all.

Just days before, we had confirmed the bombshell to my parents that I was planning to quit my career and we were going to take the kids out of school to go travelling without any end date in sight or any real itinerary set in place.

Oh, and all without a source of income.

So, yeah, naturally some questions were inevitably going to be raised over the course of the evening and, sadly, the night ended on a bad note with me getting very animated as I felt I needed to defend myself and our decision.

I felt completely untrusted and misunderstood.

What I can now look back on and see is that by the time we actually started telling friends and family of what we planned to do, we had already done the groundwork.

The research had been done, we had found the

validation, we were clear in our minds about what we wanted and why we wanted it. We had lived through the sleepless nights worrying about what might be. Thousands of different scenarios had run through our minds.

Could we come back if we didn't like travelling? Would we go broke? Would I ever get another job if I needed one? Would the kids be missing their formative years? Would our actions damage their education? Would it push them back for years? What about their friends? What about our friends? Was all of this just a pipe dream? Should we just forget it all and get on with life as we knew it?

We had been through everything, every last detail, but of course nobody else knew that.

On the face of it, when we began announcing our plans, we looked like two very irresponsible parents who were subjecting their children's lives and well-being to our own whims and fancies. I get that now, and I wish circumstances could have been handled better, by me especially.

However, every question we were asked about our decision by incredulous family or friends mounted up one by one. It sometimes felt as though we were being judged and ridiculed by those who we thought would be supportive and understanding. In reality, they were simply worried and were trying with all their might to understand what the hell was going on in our minds!

If we told 100 people, it felt like seventy-five were against the idea. Perhaps that was just perception, but perception is everything. It got to the point that I would rather not talk about it, as I was really getting down about the negative reactions.

> **"Change will not come if we wait for some other person or some other time. We are the ones we've been waiting for. We are the change that we seek."**
> - Barack Obama

When we did receive positive reactions, it was a huge booster. Someone actually got what we were trying to achieve! It was extremely gratifying when they would congratulate us for pursuing such an immensely brave life dream.

"What an adventure this will be! You will learn and see so much. You will forever look back on this time in your life and be thankful that you had the courage to carry this through. The kids will be fine, children are so adaptable and they will benefit from it so much. How many other kids get this wonderful opportunity?"

I remember clearly when some friends came over for dinner one evening after we had made 'the decision' and gave us the exact validation we needed. They knew that I had been reading 'the book' as we had spent a week in Bali with them for the New Year's holiday whilst I was on my fifth read.

As we greeted them at the door, they looked at us and paused. "Wait, what's different?" they said.

"Huh, what do you mean?"

"Something is different. What is it? You look different or feel different. Something is weird. Good, but weird."

Clearly, the magnitude of actually making the decision had had a huge effect on our personas. The dark clouds of doubt had been whisked away and the sun had finally begun to shine in full force. Seemingly, this emotion was emitting itself physically and noticeably to close friends who could pick up on our new energy immediately.

Once we told them that in the interim between last seeing them we had 100% made the decision, they were astonished.

"Wow, it's crazy how different you look. Light, happy, I don't know how to describe it. But clearly having made the decision has had a huge impact on you both!"

Telling the kids was easier. Sure, we got some push back about missing their friends, but that was pretty much their only argument. Selling the dream of 'you don't have to go to school' seemed to override that objection pretty quickly.

Besides, in the age of technology, staying in touch with friends is as easy as a Skype, FaceTime, Instagram, Tweet, Email, Message, Vine, Snapchat, WhatsApp, Line, Viber ... where does it end?

The underlying message here is this: You can't estimate how people are going to react and you need to be prepared to answer the same questions 100 times over and keep a cool head. It's easy to snap or doubt yourself if you feel challenged. Try to be patient and understand that each new person you tell will likely respond with a lot of disbelief and, sometimes, personal accusations.

Other travelling families I have spoken to about this have all experienced something similar. Some of their family and friends have even felt disdain towards them, as if they were leaving their country behind, doing it a disservice, and not being fair to their friends or their family. Many had been made to feel like they were selfish; 'Who the hell did they think they were to believe that they were so special that they could operate outside the system as they fancied?'

This is 100% a situation you will have to face if you decide to change your life so dramatically, let alone travel long-term with your children.

I wholly recommend you prepare some basic answers before informing others of your decision. Have them ready, deliver them in a cool, calm and collected manner, and be prepared for some very personal questions or assumptions directed your way.

The Hangover

"By failing to prepare, you are preparing to fail."
- Benjamin Franklin

Preparation doesn't end here, though, I am afraid. (But who said this process was going to be easy?) You will also need to prepare for the hangover!

Yes, as ridiculous as it seems, you will suffer a hangover from the old life you have purposefully escaped. Throughout our travels, this topic has come up several times and is shared equally by both sexes. In the 'family travel community', we coin the term 'Loss of Identity'.

It generally takes one or two months to set in. At first, everything is amazing. You are walking on Cloud 9! You have escaped whatever it was that was trapping you, and it feels like an elephant has just stood up and removed itself from your chest. You feel physically and mentally lighter and happier. You have time to do fun stuff with the kids -- read, walk, swim, watch movies, paint, write or whatever it is you rediscover that you actually love doing!

However, after a while, the anxiety starts creeping up on you. Your monkey brain suddenly realises that what it thought was the usual annual family vacation has seemed to overrun by a week or two. Something must be wrong.

Your mind starts telling you that you are lazy, weak, useless, not contributing to society and that other people think you are a loser for not having a title such as 'Head Of', 'VP', 'Director', 'Partner', or whatever other crap buzz word titles companies have invented to dangle over our collective heads.

To throw more gas on the fire (not to mention, completely shatter one of our original fears), in our case, job opportunities began flowing in from the moment we left. Even today, each time an offer comes in, we have to think very long and hard about the decision because every bone in my body tells me to get back in, get back to where things are safe, get back to a wage, get back to a purpose and get back to an identity!

It still happens. Even after almost three years, I still have days when I feel I need to be in an office driving something forward, in a meeting, on a business trip, on a cold call, closing a deal or being out at a client dinner or cocktail event in a hotel bar.

I suffered horribly with my 'loss of identification' after a month or two of leaving my cosy corporate world. I had no way of turning off the inner demons. And I didn't even have a title of any sort in the first place! I was just 'a broker'. Whilst travelling through France, we met a man and his family that had also quit life and travelled for some months before settling in the French countryside with his wife and two young daughters.

The guy had walked away from a high-powered title role for a large bank in Melbourne and was still trying to get his thoughts straight. We talked at length about how it's so hard to completely switch off from the life you used to live. The stresses and pressures made us feel important, and closing business deals made us feel powerful.

It was great to be able to connect with somebody who had come from the same industry and was going through the same emotions. We set up weekly calls to make sure we had an outlet if we needed one. To this day, we talk over new ideas, about his coaching business, my path to finding a new way to support my family, our experiences and investments in time or money, our overall mindset and philosophies, oh and lots of general banter.

This outlet has proven to be key for us both. It's something I recommend we all seek to foster with somebody we meet or already know who has done the same thing that we are considering.

Beyond these weekly chats, the way I deal with my anxiety now is to tell myself the following:

> *If you have some unfinished business in the corporate world, it can wait. There is no reason you can't walk back into a company at age fifty and still work for twenty years from there.*
>
> *For now, this is your job, this is your career and it is the most important one you will ever have in your life. Plus, sadly, it will only last another ten to fifteen years in its current state.*
>
> *Be the best father you can be to your children, be around for them as much as you possibly can, do as much with them as you possibly can, leave nothing on the table, and put every ounce of energy into this project!*

Once I have thought or said this aloud to somebody, the monkey brain goes quiet again. It also quiets the odd doubter or hater when they start questioning you about your life choices.

Reversing the Mindset

Change is the law of life. And those who look only to the past or present are certain to miss the future.
- John F Kennedy

How have I managed to change my mindset since leaving the corporate world?

A complete 180 is the answer.

It's been three years away from an office and corporate environment now and -- although I still have pulls to be back in a business role -- my overriding instinct is a total aversion to ever being part of that world again.

The best way I can sum up my view of the corporate world after three years of freedom is with the following analogy:

I now see skyscraping offices as nothing but glorified jails. I see old-style CEOs as prison wardens, HR managers as jailhouse sheriffs, and your direct manager as the guy walking up and down the corridor swinging the prison cell keys on his finger. He has a nightstick and will use it, banging on the bars of your cubicle to make sure you have your head down and fingers moving across a keyboard.

I see a necktie as a noose that you are forced to tie for your own execution should the time come. Those nice cufflinks you have I see as handcuffs. And, in my eyes, that hugely expensive pin striped suit you just bought from Hugo Boss may as well be a government issued orange jumpsuit.

I see home time as visiting hours, where you are temporarily allowed to spend precious little time with your loved ones, always left wanting more before being dragged back onto the chain gang of a packed train full of other poor souls destined for another day of the same old pointless grind.

I see vacations as a meagre parole that lasts a maximum of ten-fourteen days that is only rewarded to you for good behaviour. After that, you're straight back to the cell pal! We aren't finished with you yet! You're in for life, remember? Or at least until we don't need you anymore.

I see that brand new $700 smart phone you carry around as an electronic ankle bracelet that your jailors use to register any form of communication you might dare to make, and track your every movement.

I see KPIs as tallies on a jail cell wall and contracts as signing your own death warrant.

This doesn't have to be your life sentence. Times are changing.

Consider the new world of business. The tech startups of Silicon Valley are not just a whim, their methods and models of business are spreading extremely quickly across the globe. I have seen it with my own eyes. During our travels, I actively sought out office visits for the family and loved showing the kids a sneak peak of the world that waits for them.

We have been inside the belly of the beast, touring Googleplex and visiting tech companies such as Weebly and Zoosk in San Francisco. We have visited the Love Home Swap offices as a family, as well as other tech startups such as City Pantry in London.

Having seen the unorthodox techniques in action, I was blown away and wanted to be a part of it. I have recently launched an advisory business and act as a consultant, strategist and sales mentor to startup businesses who are eager to connect with some 'old world' knowledge to learn tools and tactics of how to grow their bottom lines.

Through this coaching and connectivity, I am seeing companies engaging with a young and smart workforce. I have advised many twenty-somethings in all areas of business and have been impressed with their level of engagement, hunger and ability to think outside the box.

I see young founders handing huge responsibility to their young workforce, forcing them to think fast, put projects together, run teams, identify markets, make huge judgement calls and help define the company strategy and key messages.

These young hungry professionals come to work in whatever they want to wear, they meet for morning yoga sessions on roof tops, bring pets to work, are fed team lunches and, have influential speakers invited in. Startups are congregating in co-shared workspaces to help fuel the passion and feel of dynamism, companies are helping each other grow, even swapping staff if there is a naturally better fit in a different area. I see people having fun, dammit!

It has made me feel overwhelmingly optimistic for the future hopes of the generation that will come of age and walk into these newly established businesses in ten-fifteen years' time. Namely, the generation that includes my own kids. I naturally have a huge interest in the opportunities that will be offered to them in the next decade or so.

If I can see and feel what is coming, what is changing and what will be needed, then I can help shape, guide and ready them for what lies ahead. I can encourage them to start their own businesses in sectors or areas of business that still haven't made the change, giving them greater autonomy and satisfaction from their work. Or I can help them identify good and wholesome companies where they can work.

I believe the new business horizon will play out steadily along these lines and we can eventually say goodbye to the old-style corporates, for they will become a thing of the past, a distant memory. Companies will have to change or they will find themselves
unable to even dream about attracting the talent they once had queuing at their doors.

So, yes, in summary, my mindset has changed completely, but it never would have changed if I was still sat in that same chair doing that same thing day in, day out. I had to break away to see it, and thank goodness I did.

In fact, I now see the 'comfort zone' as the 'uncomfort zone'. Think about it, most likely 99% of the people you know live within their comfort zones, but spend pretty much the whole time moaning about the same old things, time after time. What's comfortable about that? I now fear the 'comfort zone.' It makes me anxious and that I am not growing or learning. It makes me feel confined and unhappy. I am much happier outside those confines!

Rediscovery

> **"We wear the mask that grins and lies,
> It hides our cheeks and shades our eyes…"**
> - Paul Laurence Dunbar

Another strange phenomenon you will face if you step away from your current life into the wide blue yonder is a paradox of choice and a rediscovery of who you actually are. It is not a case of one door closes and another one opens; rather, it is a case of one door closes and 1000s of other doors open. In fact, if you take a step back and look left and then right, you will see that every single door along the whole length of the damn corridor has opened!

This, again, will fill you with a sense of panic and anxiety as you suddenly realise that you have no rudder, no safety line, and no guide. But remember, the guides that you are used to are not guides at all, more likely they are unsympathetic passive aggressive bosses or colleagues who are steering you the way they need you to be steered to best suit themselves.

The rudder isn't a rudder at all, rather a set of blinkers to keep you from straying too far from your given task, and the safety line you fleetingly catch hold of is actually just attached to the dangled carrot you are desperately reaching for.

We become so conditioned whilst in this arena that we end up believing that anything else is unsafe, impractical, and risky and your mind runs wild with this narrative once you have stepped away from it.

To prepare for this, I would suggest mind calming techniques such as mindfulness and meditation. Now, please don't get me wrong, I spent eighteen years of my career denouncing this (and yoga for that matter) as total hippy crap for losers who weren't busy enough with real jobs as I cracked on trying to bag the next big deal. But I wish I could go back now and apply just ten minutes a day of sitting in a quiet room to let my mind unwind. It makes total sense and I can't believe it's such a hard sell to ask people to just sit still and relax. You see what slaves we have become!

The best app and website I have been exposed to for mindfulness and meditation techniques is www.Headspace.com, which was founded by Andy Puddicombe who describes Headspace as "A gym membership for your mind." Download the app and take ten sessions of ten minutes for free. What's to lose?

You get to watch a few cartoons explaining the techniques and Andy's soothing voice talks you through every step of the way. Ten minutes disappears in an instant, leaving you energised, relaxed and ready to face the day with a clear mind.

Stepping away from your old life is also crucial in helping you rediscover and learn about who you actually are. Wait, does that sound too freaky and hippy again?

Let me explain. During our careers, we are

conditioned, shaped and formed to blend into our surroundings to be accepted by managers, colleagues and customers. We change the way we dress, our beliefs, our behaviour, the way we talk and the way we interact with people. In short, we wear an invisible mask and attempt to hide any deficiencies or a socially perceived unacceptable past.

For example, I once asked a colleague what his 'thing' was, what made him tick when he was growing up. We all have a story to tell and there is something in our past that used to set us alight. He responded that when he was growing up, he had been really into inline skating street hockey, (pretty niche huh!). In fact, he had become so good at it that he was made captain for the Great British team and toured all over the country and Europe playing in tournaments.

I was stunned with how he had excelled at a sport that he loved and clearly shown so much passion to be named country captain at such a high level!

However, the other guys listening were quick to pounce and completely ridiculed him and his sport, totally undermining his achievements. Sadly, I must say, I promptly joined the majority and took (an albeit harmless and friendly) pleasure in needling him about it, too.

He let the mask slip and paid the price of ridicule.

I wore my own mask to cover up what I perceived to be a huge flaw in my intellect.

I was a very average student at school. The classic Mr. Middle-of-the-Road. I achieved no greatness, no A's ever, hell, no B's ever. I was Mr. C at best and could never break out of that mould. No matter how much time or effort I ever put in, it always came back with maximum C and perhaps a half of a house point for my efforts.

Except for Mathematics. Maths was different. Fairly or not, I had been deemed hopeless at maths and placed into an even lower class ranking. To make matters worse, I had an awful teacher. He was ancient, wore coke bottle glasses, stunk of cigarette smoke, was balding but growing long grey straggly hair around his ears, and wore the same horrid suit and tie every day.

You know, the kind of guy that despised having to teach the lower set groups, who sneered at your every mistake and looked at you like you were a total dimwit.

I clearly remember him turning to me one lesson after marking some of my work on fractions and asking me, "Are you thick or something?"

Total humiliation in front of the class. How, then, did I ever get a career in finance?

Luckily for me, the prerequisite for becoming a trainee dog's body at a foreign exchange brokerage was to have a personality rather than a long list of degrees and honours from a business school. If you lasted the torture and menial tasks of getting breakfasts, lunches, snacks and coffees (for what turned out to be three years), then you were deemed worthy and given a shot at handling some customers.

What math I needed to know I learnt on the job as quickly as I could and always had a calculator on hand. I spent eighteen years totally shitting myself of ever being asked to do a sum in my head or looking as though I hadn't understood something. But it turned out that I wasn't that bad at maths, once I understood what I needed to do and why.

In short, I wore a mask and faked it every day.

When you are set free from this kind of existence, you slowly start unravelling your real personality and naturally start feeling happier. You let the mask slip and rediscover who you are and what you like.

My wife was shocked at how much I changed in a very short amount of time after we began travelling. The biggest change of which was talking to people. I never used to talk to people I didn't know. I didn't have time, I was busy, I had things on my mind, and I had deals to think about, customers to look after and bosses to please. I had enough friends and didn't need any more. I was totally closed off to exploring the opportunity of a dinner out with some random people she had got talking to at the playground, or meeting our kids' friends' parents for coffee on a Sunday morning.

God no!

However, without even trying, I have somehow pulled a complete 180-degree turn. Now, she can't stop me talking to random people and has to drag me away from social events. It turns out, I actually really like meeting new people and am truly interested in hearing their stories, connecting with them, arranging dinners or meet-ups and inviting them into other circles of friends we might know.

Be prepared to rediscover your real self. It's awesome!

The process of rediscovery, however, is not a solo journey for family travellers. Be prepared to discover an entirely new relationship turf that will either grant or demand a greater depth to your marriage relationship.

One of the most common questions my wife has been asked over the years, funny enough, goes something along the lines of, "How on earth do you put up having him around all day? Doesn't he drive you crazy?"

This is no exaggeration, Clair has been asked this question many times by female friends.

It's kind of crazy to think that somebody wouldn't want their loved one around them as much as possible, but modern life has defined the fact that we actually rarely ever see our spouses. Too often, both spouses (or one or the other) are employed in jobs that demand long-focused working days.

Oftentimes, work comes home and is carried out on a laptop late into the night or weekends, or worse, business trips need to be taken for up to a week or more at a time. The result is a fractured relationship, one which slowly drifts apart and too often ends in a split. All for the sake of a pushy asshole boss demanding more and more effort from you so that they can keep pushing their own agendas and scaling the company ladder!?

Of course, there are times that we drive each other nuts. That is just natural. No relationship is a bed of roses, they just don't exist. What we do know is that we would rather be together than apart as much as possible during this hugely important time in our family's lives.

If this really is a worry for you, there are steps you can take to head off any arguments and help you understand the opposite sex because, let's face it, we are completely different animals. The best advice I can offer as a man is to park your ego and don't take everything so personally. Not every comment or statement is an attack on your manhood or your ability to provide for your family.

Sadly, our monkey brain is still programmed the way it was since we started walking upright and we are prone to get defensive and introspective extremely quickly. I found a good source of information on this during a month-long home swap at a villa in Spain. Sitting on the bookshelf was a copy of *Men Are From Mars, Women Are From Venus* by John Gray. I figured, 'What the hell, I may as well have a quick look and see if it's worth reading.'

I read the book in a matter of days and still reference the lessons in my mind when I feel myself falling into a typical bad 'man habit'. It's definitely worth checking out, especially if you are about to start spending all day together!

There are many questions and situations that you will have to deal with as you prepare to exit normal life and embrace an entirely new one. You will face questions and judgmental family, friends and strangers. You will likely face your own questions, doubts, loss of identity and forced adjustments along the way as well.

Just realise that all of this is a small price for the kind of life you are creating, not only for yourself but also for your children and all those you inspire. Once you overcome the knee-jerk reaction to ask yourself what in the world you are doing, you'll discover freedom and adventure on the other side. It's a world of possibilities you never knew was waiting for you.

An All Too Common Tale

In contrast, I recently met a guy by the swimming pool of a condominium we were home swapping in whilst in Singapore. Our conversation was just further validation to back up our 'crazy' decision.

After initial handshakes and introductions, he explained to me how he had just quit his career of twenty-nine years to take a sabbatical. He then went on to tell me how he had been waiting for ages to do it, but that he had needed to keep working until his son graduated. With that worry off his mind, he had pulled the pin on work and was taking a well-earned rest.

He then went on to tell me that his son had moved to Sydney straight after graduation to chase a career and that his daughter-in-law still worked a full week in the city.

I congratulated him on his retirement and wished him well with his new life of calm and relaxation, but left feeling really sorry for his impending loneliness. Just as he was getting off the treadmill to spend more time with his son, his son was getting on ... full speed ahead.

Isn't this all too much of a common tale? We wait and wait for that magic day, or to hit that mystic target amount of money so we can enjoy life 'one day', whilst sacrificing everything that is dear to us at that specific time in life.

Ask yourself, isn't it time to just reach out and take the reins? Isn't it time to choose life?

— — — — — — — — — — — —

Thoughts From Clair

Like Dan, I also felt a loss of identity. In Singapore, I was the "Busy Expat Wife, the Stay-at-Home Mum". That was who I was and who I (hopefully) was respected for.

Initially, when we started our journey, I did feel a little lost not knowing my exact role in life, or in our family. Suddenly, everything had changed. Being with my husband full-time was wonderful. I had the best person in the world to help me out with our children; someone with the same values and ethics and views on discipline and who cared for them as much as I do.

But the way that our life had been set up before meant that I was pretty much solo parenting the children day-to-day. Of course, Dan was a hands-on dad at weekends and when he got home from work in the evenings. And he was always there when needed for emergencies. But I was the one making the day-to-day decisions. What they ate, when they ate, how they were disciplined, what they were allowed to do or how.

My decisions might not have been right all the time, but with no time to think about them or no one to second guess them, I had always acted in whatever way I thought best and moved on.

Now, however, Dan was around ALL OF THE TIME

and he made decisions for the kids that may not have always been how I would have handled things. This was difficult at first to get used to. Dan was stricter than me on some things (for example, their diet and sugary treats), and other times I was stricter than Dan (for example, iPad time).

It didn't take long for the kids to know to ask me for certain things and Dan for others! It also created some friction between the two of us when the other felt that the situation should have been handled differently. With time, Dan and I learnt to communicate better with each situation as it arose.

Then, when we stopped full-time travel and settled for a while in France, I felt that I couldn't use the "Full-time Travelling Mum of Four" identity either. And I started to feel a little lost again because I wasn't able to connect or create with a new identity. It's strange because they are just identities and labels and we shouldn't get hung up on them, but I did mourn them nonetheless.

I did, however, hope that I would discover more about myself during our travels and rediscover who I am.

Since I didn't have a moment to think about who I was in my old daily routine, I hoped to discover new likes, interests and hobbies. And I have! I have uncovered a love for history (that was dampened at school) and an interest for the environment, responsible tourism, healthy eating (and learning about better nutrition and farming practices), and a special interest in clean beauty and hygiene products that don't harm our environment or our bodies. And I am far more spiritual now that we have the time to think deeper about everyday things.

We also found that some things were a little difficult to sort out in our family dynamic. Firstly, we had very little or no adult alone time as we were always with the kids and had no other options for child care. We also spent every waking hour together for a very long time. This was mostly good, but every relationship has its moments -- even more so when you are with each other day in and day out.

We found one solution to this after about a year into our trip. Whilst in San Francisco, we split the family for a day and went in different directions. Dan had booked a time to fulfill a dream of his to test drive a Tesla car. He took Samuel on the train out to the show room in the suburbs and they had a boys' day out.

In the meantime, I took the girls for long overdue haircuts, went shopping and then went to get chocolate sundaes at the famous Ghirardelli ice cream parlour. When we all got home, we realised that this was the first time that we'd all been apart in a year. We had really missed each other and all had so much to talk about!

Another big discovery we have experienced as a family is one of mindset. During our travels, we have received such amazing kindness from so many people. This has given me, and hopefully all of us, a much-restored faith in humanity. It has also taught us to be better. Most notably, our children will play with other children regardless of whether they can speak the same language or not. They play with children of different religions, races and economical status.

Just last week, they were playing with a Thai boy on the beach. Our children don't speak Thai and the little boy didn't speak English. As it got late, they asked the boy, via Google translate, where his parents were and whether he was hungry. He responded via the app that his parents were working in another village and that he was hungry. So, our kids invited him to share their dinner, to which he did. Watching this play out was most heartwarming indeed!

Without doubt we have all learnt what a wonderful and beautiful world this is. Most importantly for us, it has concreted our family bonds. We definitely do not regret taking the leap.

TOOLS AND TRICKS

The listing techniques! Another technique I have found to be hugely beneficial for clearing the mind and staying focussed is that of writing a list every morning when I wake up. All of the random stuff I have dreamt up during my sleep goes straight onto that day's to-do list.

I then re-order them in importance and condense the list to roughly five things, concentrating on anything that will push us forward financially or critical things that need to be addressed, rather than kicked down the road.

"Oh yeah, great idea," I hear you say, never heard of that before!

But here is the kicker, at the end of each day, before I want to sit down and relax, read a book, watch a film or enjoy a dinner, I make another list.

I call this technique reverse listing. Take five minutes to list down all of the other random things you have done that day, and as soon as you write it down put a line straight through it. The more you can do the better, so don't feel bad about adding every little thing you might have done, even go so far as listing all of the emails you have responded to, or texts you have sent. Whatever it is, write it down and promptly cross it out before writing down the next thing.

The effect this has on the mind is incredible. After just five minutes, you will have a list as long as your arm of actions, jobs and tasks you have achieved that day. You can then enjoy your evening without the self-doubt and nagging voices in your head dragging you down.

An example of what one of my reverse lists might look like:

~~Help make kids breakfast~~
~~Take kids to school~~
~~Arrange play date~~
~~Help Clair with housework~~
~~Research next trip~~
~~Email Alex~~
~~Shower~~
~~Clean teeth~~
~~Email Scott~~
~~Email Jamie~~
~~Email Gareth~~
~~Made bank transfer~~
~~Called Mum and Dad~~
~~Cleaned car~~

~~Exercised~~
~~Skype call with Michael~~
~~Skype call with Stuart~~
~~Completed banking forms~~
~~Checked Love Home Swap responded to 4 members~~
~~Write book~~
~~Check twitter~~
~~Check Facebook~~
~~Check Gmail~~
~~Look at investments~~
~~Check stock market~~
~~Prepare lunch~~
~~Coffee with friends~~
~~Listen to podcast~~
~~Helped old lady cross road~~
~~Pick up kids~~
~~Message Jo~~
~~Organise golf~~
~~Prep dinner~~
~~Cook dinner~~
~~Make shopping list~~
~~Email Ashley~~

You get the picture. Literally, add anything you can think of at all and instantly cross it out. Then, sit back, relax and open that bottle of red. You will be left with a calm mind knowing that hey, you achieved a shitload of stuff today!

www.Headspace.com and find Andy Puddicombe on Twitter @andypuddicombe

Men Are From Mars, Women Are From Venus - John Gray.

Is something holding you back in life? You can't get that promotion, haven't started that business, haven't approached the person of your dreams, can't take a leap of faith? The reality is it's yourself that's stopping you. Steve Chapman's Ted talk introduces you to his inner critic and wears a mask to show you what he looks like. https://www.youtube.com/watch?v=lnf-

Ka3ZmOM&feature=youtu.be

Startup companies I have been privileged enough to work with:
www.citypantry.com
www.weddingplanner.co.uk
www.weengs.co.uk

I have also continued to work closely with:
www.amoriabond.com

Chapter 4
The Sharing Economy

"As people's access to the internet grows we're seeing the sharing economy boom - I think our obsession of ownership is at a tipping point and the sharing economy is part of the antidote for that."
- Richard Branson

The presenter on CTV Ottawa Consumer news announced that over two million Canadians had tried it in the last year and would consider doing it again!

I was watching a YouTube clip and no, it's not what you think! I had been searching the internet for alternative ways to travel and stumbled across the consumer study report which introduced the concept of home swapping via the sharing economy.

The clip cut to Debbie Wosskow, a British entrepreneur who had been inspired by the film 'The Holiday' starring Cameron Diaz and Kate Winslet. After watching the movie, an idea sparked in her mind to set up her own home swapping company. She was a single mother of two who loved to travel, but found that the usual experience of hotel rooms wasn't working anymore. She had been left huddled in the corner of her hotel room with the TV turned all the way down, eating room service each night after the kids had fallen asleep, too many times.

Hardly comfortable and hardly a holiday.

In the clip, she explained that the average cost saving for a holiday using her home swapping service was into the thousands of dollars per trip as families exchange their homes and sometimes cars. It also opens up the opportunity to take trips to parts of the world that you might not have even considered before as the company was global and growing.

I needed more information. I Google searched Debbie's name and watched more and more clips from her press junkets out of the U.S., Australia and the UK.

The message was clear: Home swapping was on the rise and it was a unique and affordable way to travel. We were at the cutting edge of a huge change in collective thinking.

Services like Airbnb and Couchsurfing were catching the attention of people who wanted and needed a change to the usual travel experience. The travel industry at large was about to experience a huge awakening.

"Amandla Awethu!"
"Power to the people!"

Little did I know at this point of early home swapping researching that we would end up swapping over sixty-five times across four continents in more than fifteen different countries, all via the sharing economy for two and a half years straight!

Many of you reading this book are homeowners, of which, many of you are also likely to own a second home. To those lucky enough to be in either position, you cannot underestimate the power you hold in your hands to the fellow traveller. Hell, even if you are renting you can still host home swappers, couch surfers or Help (more later on this) volunteers offering their services in exchange for a roof over their heads and often a meal. You can still become part of the travel community and get exposure to many people from all walks of life who inspire you with their stories and free energy.

I have talked at length about home swapping with many people along our journey and have inspired some to try it themselves. However, the majority remain skeptical and fearful, unable to overcome trusting another human being in their home.

How far has humanity fallen? How often have you ever vandalised property or stolen something of value to somebody else? I am assuming never! So why, then, would you assume the complete opposite of somebody else?

Why has society fallen into this protective state of not trusting anybody around us? Many would argue that it is the fault of mainstream news media, which is now basically controlled by a very few, very rich individuals who care nothing about us or anyone else and even control our politicians.

Whether this is true or not, this fear of the fellow human being who is out for themselves, looking to take something from you or screw you over is prevalent in society and really needs to be addressed.

Honestly, people are pretty damn cool, just give them a chance to prove it. I guarantee that you will be bowled over by the kindness you receive in return for simply asking somebody for help.

When was the last time you stopped and asked somebody for directions?

Try it. Watch the response on that person's face and feel the sense of gratification they get when you say thank you and smile at them. If you still have your doubts about humanity, read on! In just a minute we'll discuss some of the bigger questions I get about home swapping.

For now, consider that one of the great benefits of the sharing economy is that you are not only the recipient of others' generosity, but you are also one of the generous individuals restoring others' faith in humanity.

"In spite of everything, I still believe that people are really good at heart."
- Anne Frank

Slashing Travel Costs

It was recently reported that the average British family spends up to two months' salary on their summer holiday break, a good percentage of that cost being spent on accommodation. This seems crazy!

You will be happy to know that home swapping provides another way.

You can leverage your own house or holiday home

and travel to other wonderful destinations and stay in the most amazing houses, villas, flats or apartments. And all of this for free if you're willing to allow other people to stay in your house in return.

This is exactly what we did and still do with the aforementioned www.lovehomeswap.com, and it has proven to be an awesome experience.

Home exchange is not a new concept, but like most other businesses, social networking on the internet has bought it a whole new lease of life.

Listing your home on the site is easy and, best of all, free. Yes, FREE. All you do is upload some pictures of your property with a description about the house and yourselves, hit the upload button, sit back and wait!

Needless to say, the better the pictures and the more descriptive the narrative, the more interest you will get, so put a little effort in early.

One key caveat is that once you connect with people that are interested in swapping with you and are ready to start exchanging dates and details etc., you will have to become a paying member of the site. The basic package is all one needs to get started. Prices start from around 15 GBP per month. We still use this package and have enjoyed excellent service from the team in charge of our account. That is a hell of a saving on your accommodation fees!

After just two weeks of being listed, we had received two swap requests — from France and Switzerland — and had been shortlisted by three other members and received over thirty views.

Home Swapping FAQs

There are, of course, many questions that people want answered before they start sharing their homes. Let's drill down into the main objections I hear from people when I mention home swapping to them.

"But what if they just trash your house?"

Let's be totally honest here, things are going to break

from time-to-time and accidents will happen. Luckily, whilst we have stayed at other members homes, we have only ever had to deal with a dropped glass, plate or bowl (perhaps plural).

In those situations, we simply emailed the owner and let them know what happened and to ask where we can buy a new one to replace it. They always come back with a response of, "Don't worry about it, it's a glass. Who cares?!"

There was also the time a shower hose broke, it was no fault of ours. It had just come to the end of its lifespan. I emailed the owner, explained what happened and asked where the nearest DIY store was. I had it fixed in no time.

We have had situations in our home that have left some small damage too, but again, that all just comes with wear and tear and is to be expected. For the most part, we have found that folks in the home swapping community are far more respectful than paying renters. In fact, after talking to many of the members, we have found that this feeling corresponds with lots of people's experiences on the site.

It comes down to a question of psychology. When people pay to rent a property, they feel a much greater sense of ownership, whereas a home swapper feels a huge sense of stewardship. The home swappers mindset is completely different, they feel a connection to the person they are swapping with as they have already had lots of contact with them leading up to the swap. Plus, they feel a sense of responsibility to keep the house clean and in good working order.

We always do a full clean of the house prior to departure and leave a welcome home note to the owners. We have always received nothing but good responses and have been happy with the way our property and belongings have been treated, too.

I guess as humans we are just trained to fear the worst, but let's take a step back and actually think about it. The people you have conversed with are also paying members of the site, they are already like-minded people with similar ethics and outlook on life, just a little extra faith in humanity is all that's needed. People don't want to ruin your things and they aren't going to steal from you either!

"But why would anybody want to stay here?"

This is a classic response and one you will find comes up over and over if you decide to home swap, house sit, couch surf or whatever it is you are doing.

The truth is, you have no idea why or when people will need to be in your vicinity. Maybe they have family in the area but have nowhere to stay, a job interview nearby, short term work to conduct in the area, a profound love of your area, a wedding, a funeral, a party, the list of reasons is endless.

Try and stay positive and not fall into the trap of underestimating the value that you and your location could offer to somebody else.

I was once interviewed by a young reporter from The Sun newspaper in London. He was astonished by the home swapping stories we told and that we were actually talking to him directly from a home swap in New Zealand that had direct access to a lake and kayaks for us to use.

At the end of the interview he surmised, "Well it's all very nice for you, but nobody will ever want to swap with me!"

I decided to challenge him. He lived in a small flat located on the east side of London. I made him a bet that he couldn't refuse to take. These were the rules I asked him to follow:

Take some nice pictures of your tidy flat, add a descriptive narrative about the surrounding area, the pubs, restaurants, transport system into Central London, the parks and sites of interest nearby. Tell people a little about yourself, your job, what you like about the area, what football teams are nearby and who you support, what events are coming up in London and why you are looking to swap, etc.

He then had to list his flat on Love Home Swap, which is free. The terms of the bet were simple: if he was not approached within two weeks of listing his property, I would pay him twenty pounds. If he was approached within two weeks, then he would pay nothing. I would win just by the pure happiness of hooking him up with a potential holiday.

In good spirit, he decided to do it and followed the rules. I received a message from him four days after he had fully uploaded his profile and pictures onto the site:

"Have you been paying people off to make me swap

offers?! Had none until today at which point I received three. Although two were for non-simultaneous (which we couldn't do yet) and one was for at least three months! But maybe something workable there. Make that four!!!"

My money was safe!

> **You must not lose faith in humanity. Humanity is an ocean; if a few drops of the ocean are dirty, the ocean does not become dirty.**
> - Mahatma Gandhi

"What if the swap falls through?"

Now, as much as I have painted the perfect picture of a home swapping lifestyle, there are, of course, instances when swaps don't work out perfectly and might even get cancelled before arrival. This could be due to lots of reasons. For example, a family who were due to visit our house in December decided to cancel because the island had suffered some bad flooding and they didn't want to risk ruining their holiday with bad weather.

We respected their wishes and simply rearranged another time for them to visit the house.

Another example is of a family who wanted to swap with us long term, giving us the opportunity of living in Kent, England for three months over the Christmas period. However, after a few months into their round-the-world trip, a health issue arose and they had to return home and subsequently cancel our upcoming swap.

This, of course, was a bit of a worry as we were due to arrive in just two months and now had no accommodation booked! But we got onto the Love Home Swap site and started approaching as many people as we could. In just a few days, we managed to line up three separate one-month-long swaps in different regions of the UK, we still spent a great three months there and got to see a lot more of the country by staying in three different counties.

If you would feel more comfortable with the knowledge that you are protected against cancellations, there are different insurance policies available on the Love Home Swap site and I am sure this is most likely the case for all of the other home exchange sites out there too. If you want that extra peace of mind, then look into the right policy for you and your situation.

I don't want these last examples to dampen your interest in researching home swapping as an option for your travel. However, it's important to highlight that yes, sometimes plans, for whatever reason, can simply go wrong. Be that as it may, it's also important to remember that this is true with conventional travel too.

How often has a flight been delayed or canceled? Is it impossible for a hotel to suffer flood or other damage due to inclement weather conditions, burst pipes, or other maintenance issues that create bad smells and lots of noisy and unsightly repair work? Sometimes booking systems go haywire or an internet site has double booked the hotel and there is no room available for you on arrival.

The list of possibilities is endless. The trick is to adjust your mindset to the fact that hiccups of some kind can happen along the way and to just roll with it when it happens.

"We rent our apartment, so we wouldn't be allowed to list it."

Yes, I understand your concerns here, but it might be worth you looking at it from a slightly different angle. Would the landlord really care?

For home swapping, it's easy to overcome this worry as you aren't exchanging money. On the face of it, you aren't directly profiting from somebody staying in your house. There is no tangible financial gain. I am sure that in the past you have invited friends and family to stay with you, the only difference here is that you aren't around and on hand to drive them to all of the tourist places they would like to visit because you are away on your own travels!

However, it is possible to make tangible cash from your property (rented or owned) through other travel websites. My friend's story is the perfect example to highlight the arguments for and against such an approach.

Many people list their properties via sites such as Airbnb and are, in fact, making some money to help with their incomes and pay the landlord his rent. Perhaps they have a spare bedroom to loan out, or they are going on holiday themselves and list the dates on the site as available when the apartment will be empty.

My friend went one step further and listed his rented apartment on Airbnb with the thought that he would crash with a mate if he ever got an enquiry. Over the course of one year he banked $17,000.

Is this being deceitful?

Is this against the law?

Why? He paid the agreed rental to the landlord, kept the place very clean and tidy, met and looked after his guests, employed a cleaner and made himself a nice little bonus for the year.

Everybody is winning in that formula. Did the landlord even care? No. They have a full-term contracted tenant and regular payments. The fact that my friend was just a little happier and better off should have worked in the landlord's favour. Landlords love happy tenants that renew their contracts!

Now, governments of course don't like this because they want to tax you on your extra income, they believe that they should have their slice of your dollars too.

This is a huge debating point for the sharing economy at large. Here is my belief on the subject, and for ease I will keep the example focused on property. If you own a home that you are paying for (rent or mortgage) you would have likely paid stamp duty tax, state or local council taxes, pool, loft or kitchen floor taxes, driveway taxes, parking taxes, roof taxes, water, electricity and God knows whatever else taxes.

Why then, or more to the point, how then should the government be able to tax you on any income you are making from the spare bedroom you are renting out to strangers once in a while?

It's absurd!

Of course, if there is a clear way for you to report that income, then you should pay it. No reason to break the law.

Anyway, we will leave that debate alone before it gets too heated and get on with the subject of home swapping and how you could find yourself travelling to some of the most wonderful places with access to free accommodation.

Home Swapping in Action

If you are still unconvinced about the home swapping movement and how it could benefit you, then read on! Let's use two different sets of people as examples:

Jo and David are married thirty-somethings without kids who are both teachers. They get a lot of time off work over the course of the year due to the school holidays, but sadly don't have the means to scratch their travel itch as much as they could. They live in a modest three-bedroom house close to a commuter town with direct access into a city.

John and Kirsty are married forty-somethings with three kids. Both are tired of life on the treadmill and the kids are having a pretty tough time at school with all the testing and social pressures. They live in a four-bedroom house in the countryside and dream of escaping to travel for an extended period of time. John has applied for a sabbatical and has been granted two months off.

Looking to test the theories in this book about home swapping, both families join a home exchange website of their choice and start approaching other members of the home swapping community.

They tap in their dates of travel and hit the search button. Thousands of properties show up available for those dates (to trawl through them all would spin your mind).

Jo and David fancy some time in Asia, so they filter the countries of Japan and Vietnam, press search and get a hit of fifty houses or apartments that might be able to swap with them in their stated date range.

Rather than be picky and trawl through each one, they hit every single person with the same chat request. (This is by far the best approach, don't think it's rude to do this, you will likely only get ten to fifteen responses, of which, only a few will be workable.) They write:

"Hey there (name),

We hope this message finds you well!

Having just joined the site, it is safe to say that we are new to home swapping, but excited to learn more if you have any tips!

We just found your home on the site and wondered if you might be interested in arranging a swap with us.

David and I are both teachers at the local high school here where we live. Our house was recently redecorated and is situated just a twenty-minute walk from a train station with direct access to the city. We are tidy and respectful travellers and would take great pride in looking after your home whilst you are away.

You are welcome to use our bikes and car to explore the surrounding area. We also have membership to some local attractions such as castles and gardens which we could leave for you to use too.

Hope to hear from you, even if you are unable to swap!

Wishing you a great day, Jo and David

John and Kirsty decide that they would love to travel through Europe for two months, hitting as many countries as possible. They decide to filter France, Spain, Switzerland, Germany and Italy and hit search.

The results are still in the thousands, so they filter for vacation homes (this gives you a much higher rate of success as the houses are sitting empty for some parts of the year) and listings with at least three bedrooms to get down to a working list of seventy-five homes.

They then spend the evening over a bottle of wine scrolling through each listing and taking note of any reviews other travellers have left. They build a short list and feel the surge of excitement rise as they realise that this could really be possible.

After finding twenty properties, they fire off the following chat message to each one:

Dear (Name),

We are a young family looking for the adventure of a lifetime.

> *Our three kids are aged nine, eleven and thirteen. As parents, we feel that the time is now right to take them on an extended trip to open up their eyes and minds to the wonders of different cultures and history.*
>
> *John is in finance and Kirsty is a full-time mum! This is our first time home swapping, so please don't hold back with any advice or tips. ;)*
>
> *Our house is based in the wonderful countryside surrounded by rolling fields and tiny villages. The area is famous for its natural beauty and we are within easy driving distance of all amenities, an airport and train station. You would be made most welcome into the community by our neighbours and friendly village locals who would gladly share with you their knowledge of the area and be on hand to help you in any way.*
>
> *We look forward to hearing from you soon and thank you for considering our approach.*
>
> *Best regards, John, Kirsty and kids.*

The next day, Jo and David have email notifications that they have three messages waiting for them in their inbox on the site. They eagerly click through to the website and read the responses. Two are very nice responses, but sadly aren't able to work out a swap as they already have travel plans in place for this year. The third response is really interesting.

> *Dear Jo and David,*
> *So lovely to hear from you and thank you for reaching out.*
>
> *As luck would have it, we actually travel back to your area every other year to visit family. We are expats living here Japan. Since having the children, it gets harder and harder to stay with family when we visit, so this home swap sounds perfect.*
>
> *Would it be possible to give us a few days to liaise the dates with work and check airline prices etc.?*

As you can see from our listing on the website, we have swapped numerous times and are very respectful of other people's homes. I hope you read the reviews other guests have left.

We know you would love it here and can offer you train passes and the use of our Uber account if need be.

As for dates of travel, we generally leave for three weeks. Would that suit you too?

Best regards, Sarah

John and Kirsty also have some replies in their inbox and click through, eagerly reading them, but get a little disheartened by the first reply.

Dear John and Kirsty,

Sorry to say we are fully booked over the period you are looking for.

All the very best with your search and welcome to the home swapping movement!

Best regards, Dan

Pushing on to the next reply, they are met with a glimmer of hope!

Dear John and Kirsty,
Thank you for getting in touch and considering us for a swap. Your new adventure sounds thrilling, and well done to you both for taking such an amazing view to life and your children's further education.

The house we have listed on the site is unfortunately full for the dates you specified, but our main home will be free as we will be travelling ourselves over that time. It is a comfortable four bed home overlooking the lake.

You could come and stay here whilst we are gone and perhaps we could stay at your home at some other point during your extended travels?

We are fully open to discussion and quite flexible as we are retired. ;)

I really hope we can figure something out for you.

Best regards, Paul and Beverly

Et voila, both couples now have something concrete to work with and can get on to tailoring further swaps in and around their chosen target countries, building a full itinerary and saving thousands.

This is exactly how we leverage home swapping and have been amazed at the openness and responses we have received. In fact, we have even taken it off piste so to speak! We recently received the happy news of a family wedding taking place in Guernsey and, of course, needed to attend.

Not keen to pay the 300 pounds per night to a hotel for two rooms, we tried our luck to find a home swap. As Guernsey is a tiny island, there were not many swap options listed on the website and nothing was going to be available or suited to our needs.

Rather than give up, we Google searched apartments and hotels in the area and found a wonderful looking site describing themselves as an "Apart-Hotel".

We clicked through to make an enquiry through the booking system and sent the following email:

Dear (name),
We have just found your wonderful looking Apart-Hotel on the internet and wanted to reach out to you about a possible stay.

Over the weekend of the - - - we will be attending a family wedding in Guernsey and are looking at different accommodation options.

What is unique about our enquiry is that we wondered if you would like to swap your largest family apartment with us in return for a stay in our home.

We are an accomplished travelling family and have home swapped over sixty-five times on a world trip which has spanned over two-and-a-half years across four continents and over fifteen different countries.

You can find out more about us by following the link to our blog www.princesoffthegrid.weebly.com.

If you would be open to discussion, we could arrange a weeklong stay for you for free.

I understand you most likely don't get many requests like this and we are, of course, open to discussing it further by phone, Skype or FaceTime.

Best regards,

Daniel and Clair Prince

The owner responded within an hour, completely surprised by our random approach and open to learning more about the opportunity. Within a few days, we had a deal worked out and both parties were happy with the outcome.
Free holidays when and where we needed them, people talking to people and solving each other's problem.
Simple.
I then took things a step further. The drive time for us was going to be eleven hours, and the flights just didn't work out as we needed to make connections through the UK on budget airlines. I did not place a great deal of confidence in that system over such a special weekend!
I thought to myself, 'What would be the ultimate answer to this problem?'
The answer was obvious. If only we could fly ourselves. No queue, no customs, no connections, no eleven-hour drive, no fuss, no hassle.
But this was a non-starter. How could I afford to learn

to fly, then buy or rent a plane to make the trip? It was madness.

But, wait, what if…? I jumped straight onto the laptop and researched local aero clubs in our region and sent out an email to the head of the clubs with a request for any members interested in swapping their services of flying us privately in their own plane to and from Guernsey, in return for a free one week stay in our home.

It turned out in the end to be a non-starter, as well. As we are such a large family, the kind of plane we needed was up into the celebrity status G5 jet league. Beyoncé, we ain't!

We did have one couple offer to do shuttle runs to come and collect us in their three-seater plane, but it was just a little too much for them to handle in the end and rather impractical. But if we didn't ask, we would never have known!

Honestly, what risk are you taking other than another person saying no?

Why do we fear the no?

At what stage in life do we grow into fearing the no? Kids don't fear it, despite the fact that it's sometimes the only word they ever hear!

If we can all get out of our own way, stop fearing the "no" and approach people with a friendly and sincere demeanour, the world would be a much happier place and our collective lives would be much more fulfilling.

The people we have swapped with and have met in person or via Skype have been wonderful and have even become friends of the family. Travel has changed us for the better, forever.

It's also important to note that roughly 50-60% of the people we have swapped with have been from the baby boomer generation. This lifestyle is not just aimed at or available to younger generations who flit around conducting work from laptops. If you are a boomer reading this book, please understand that the property you own and the time and flexibility you have can unlock a dream retirement for you.

The sharing economy has come to life, driven by a younger generation that has been forced to think and look at life differently. But it isn't exclusive to that age range, everyone is invited!

Consider the fact that the boomer generation (approx. 1943-1965) is the biggest and wealthiest generation in history, and possibly won't be matched again. Plus, this generation holds most of the global wealth and assets.

According to one study, the British baby boomers held 80% of the UK's wealth in 2004 and bought 80% of all upscale cars, 80% of cruises and 50% of all skincare products.

With the awakening of the sharing economy and the acceptance of technology from this generation we are on the verge of an avalanche of opportunities. Imagine the doors that can be flung open with the sharing of homes, cars, tools and other goods all tied up in the boomer banks. No generation has ever amassed so much wealth, property, cars and other consumer goods. Once the realisation to the benefits of leveraging these assets sinks in, the already hugely successful sharing economy movement will be set to kick up another gear.

Returning to the focus on home swapping, its greatest benefit is freeing up the cost of accommodation. You can, at the very minimum, cut the cost of a trip in half, perhaps even more. If you can fly cheap budget airlines to the destination, or even drive there, then you are almost cost-free.

My advice, roll the dice and take those pictures, list your property and see what happens. If something comes off, that's great. You can look forward to a holiday that will give you the possibility to save loads of expenses, or look at it differently, and enjoy the extra food and wine, my friends!

You gain strength, courage, and confidence by every experience in which you really stop to look fear in the face. You must do the thing which you think you cannot do.
- Eleanor Roosevelt

More Than One Way to Share

And, if for some reason home swapping doesn't work for you, there are still plenty of other ways you can enter the sharing economy. Volunteering your time can reap huge benefits, not only for what you get in return but also for the feeling of satisfaction you gain for helping somebody in need and making that ground level connection with a complete stranger.

During our three and a half months of travel in New Zealand, we had five weeks to find accommodation as we couldn't confirm any swaps over the high summer season. We joined HelpX for NZD 20 after learning about it through some fellow travellers.

This is how it works: For four or five hours of work per day, you are provided with free accommodation and, in some cases, breakfast, lunch and dinner!

Once your work is completed, you are free to go and explore the surrounding areas, get off the beaten path, or tick off all the mainstream tourist destinations. In fact, your host will become your most trusted and personal travel guide, giving you all of the local knowledge and secret spots for you to check out.

We spent two separate weeks on two different farms and another week in an old hospital that was being renovated into a hostel. Our work ranged from gardening, washing windows and painting to cleaning, general house work and even milking 370 cows!

Each experience was completely unique and took us all out of our comfort zone and tested our mettle, all of which we found truly fulfilling. The kids had a blast, we became good friends with our hosts and learnt about their lives, family, industry and country through their own eyes. A totally different experience to staying in a hotel.

And again, all for FREE accommodation!

There is seemingly a sharing economy sector for almost everything now. For example, whilst we were in Sydney, we needed to hire a car for a weekend to visit some friends who lived a three-hour drive away.

We found and used www.carnextdoor.com.au and contacted them about their services and business model. I spoke directly to the founder of the company who had posted his own mobile number under the 'contact us' tab and he explained how it worked.

"Car owners are rarely in their cars," he said. "They sit

parked all day long and are a huge burden in running costs, servicing, insurance and tax, etc. I devised a way that people could have their car earn money for them to offset some of these costs. You simply lend your car to somebody else who pays you a fee much smaller than that of mainstream hire companies. It's a win-win situation!"

I logged into the site, put in my location and was surprised to see a choice of five different cars all within a fifteen-minute walking distance from me. I picked my car, received a text and walked to the address to find the key in the lock box, easy!

All you have to do is take pictures of the vehicle before and after and promise to return it in a clean condition.

It felt great to know that the money was going to the owner of the car — a real person, not a faceless conglomerate — and she was thrilled to make contact with us and glad we were able to visit our friends in her car.

Trust. It will open more doors in life than you could ever imagine.

A Solution for Everything

If you are travelling longer-term and plan to stay for some months in one location, you will likely need your own vehicle. The usual rental firms will end up charging you a fortune, so make sure you look at all the options open to you!

We were headed to New Zealand for several months and, at the time, had no end date planned. Asking around for advice through our travel communities, we got some good ideas and tips about car rentals and were even offered cars from travellers leaving the country. Sadly, they were in totally different locations to where we were landing.

Others informed us that they had managed to hire campervans from companies such as www.imoova.com for as little as a few dollars a day! Here is how Imoova explains their business:

> "Travel the world in relocation rentals from $1 per day. RV, camper and car rental companies sell relocation rentals through

imoova.com as a way to save money on paying drivers and trucking vehicles.

This is your opportunity to road trip in the cheapest and best way. From as little as $1 per day imoova.com will match your holiday trip and dates with vehicles needing relocation.
You can book online here from a list of available trips in Australia, NZ, USA, Canada and Europe or phone our seven-day call centre. If you cannot find what you are looking for you can join our waitlist and you will be notified by SMS and email when a match for your trip comes up."

Sadly, for us, we couldn't make any of these opportunities tie in with our movements. In the end, we opted to buy our own car and then sell it when we left. The plan was simple: land in Christchurch, rent a car for one week and get busy trawling the second-hand dealerships in town for a day to figure out our best options and prices.

The dealers were unbelievably friendly, totally the opposite of the stereotypical car dealer you see in the movies or TV programmes. These guys were going out of their way to help us and even put us in touch with their friends and competitors rather than try and force sell us a car that didn't fit our needs.

With our on-the-ground research completed, we hit the internet and, again, leveraged the sharing economy.

Trademe.co.nz is the equivalent to EBay in New Zealand. We found the perfect vehicle for our family up for auction, a Toyota Estima that could seat up to eight people and still had a ton of space for luggage. We put in our bid and waited for the next day when the auction was closing.

As we were touring around Restart mall in Christchurch, the text updates were coming in thick and fast as the minutes ticked down to the end of the auction.

Our budget was NZD 4500. This had been decided because that had been the best price we could find for the same kind of car at one of the dealerships during our on the ground research. Anything under that price would be considered a bonus in our eyes.

The auction close time drew near and we all gathered

around our iPhone waiting for the result. We knew we were in the mix because we had set our target budget and it hadn't got to that yet, but late bidders had come out of nowhere and had started raising the price!

This added another two minutes onto the auction close time. Then another counter offer, another two minutes, then another counter and another two minutes … oooooh the agony!

This happened at least five or six times and we were getting really anxious. Finally, it closed. The last bidders had been priced out! We received a final text.

We had won the auction at a cost of NZD 1900! 1900! A cost saving of NZD 2600!

I called the family selling the car to arrange a pick-up date and time. The lady was super friendly and just as excited about selling the car as we were about buying it. She then went on to explain that her family members were immigrating to Australia and were leaving from Christchurch airport the next day. She asked if it might be possible for them to use the car one last time to drive themselves to their motel where we could meet them to exchange keys for cash.

Of course we could! It was just fifteen minutes from where we were staying. They practically delivered the car to us!

They were a lovely family. We spent some time getting to know them and hearing their story about immigrating to start a new life in Australia. It turned out that they had even sold their house on the website too at a huge cost saving compared to estate agent and legal fees.

The car was perfect. She toured us around the whole of both islands of New Zealand and never skipped a beat. All of us could have shed a tear saying goodbye to such a loyal servant, but come the day we left Auckland for San Francisco, I drove Scuttlebug (the wife and kids named her) into an auction house and sold her on the spot for NZD 1000 cash.

In all it amounted to a total cost of NZD 900 to own and drive our car around NZ for three and a half months!

"Ah yes, BUT," I hear you all cry, "What about insurance costs!"

In New Zealand, it is not law to buy insurance for your car. We opted not to. Considering you sometimes see three cars during a five-hour road trip, we thought we might play the odds!

Of course, all decisions are personal and up to each individual to decide their best course of action in these and all circumstances.

House Sitting

> "Wherever you go, go with all your heart."
> - Confucius

House sitting is another travel sharing economy phenomenon, and one we have also used as we travelled extensively throughout France. There are numerous sites out there offering house sits and you can easily sign up for free trials to see how lucky you can get. We have met families that have house sat their way around the world for years.

This is how it works: Many people own second homes in different countries that they seldom use. Lots of these people prefer not to rent out their properties to paying guests as it incurs costs with management and cleaning fees, agent and advertising fees and taxes on received rental income within the country in question. Rather than rent out their homes, the homeowners join the house-sitting sites as hosts and offer their homes to people who are looking for accommodation in that country.

The idea is simple: You are expected to look after the general upkeep of the property in return for a roof over your head.

Our experience of house sitting couldn't have been better, or more fun! We found a house in central France on Nomador.com that was owned by a British guy who needed the garden looked after while he was unable to be there.

For two months, we lived in his house, taking great care and pride in our surroundings. We weeded the whole driveway and flower beds, cleaned out the pond, planted an herb garden, re-chipped some walkways, mowed the lawn, trimmed bushes, pruned trees, set rat, mole and mice traps, collected post and dealt with builders, plumbers and electricians.

We kept the house running smoothly and reported any problems as they arose so that the owner had a clear picture of what was happening with the house in his absence. Everything was at his cost and he was more than eager to send money to our bank account to cover the costs for any materials or tools we needed to complete any work.

During our time, we also got to take many day trips to explore the surrounding area and became very friendly with the neighbours, which made us feel really at home, even if we couldn't understand each other!

> **"Tourists don't know where they've been, travellers don't know where they're going."**
> - Paul Theroux

Just the Beginning

There are countless different ways you can get creative to fund your travels and enhance every step you take.

For instance, along our journeys I met Alex of Foodishboy.com and was amazed by his experience. Alex set himself the goal of travelling around the world by working in a different kitchen for each week of the year. Alex nailed it and during one year worked in fifty-two different kitchens in twenty countries across four continents.

Enter Alex:

> *The world was my classroom and the greatest chefs and producers it's teachers. I mastered the art of fermentation in Japan, nixtamalization in Mexico and saucier skills in Vietnam. I farmed organic produce in California, learned about seasonality through Nordic eyes and got to grips with the unrivalled kitchen pantry supplied by Peru's varied topography. The fields of Mendoza educated me in viniculture, the Brazilian jungle, tutored me in coffee harvesting and the pastures of Sicily gave extra tutelage in cheese making.*
>
> *From Michelin-starred restaurants to fish and chip shops, from*

> *coffee farms in Brazil to tea plantations in Darjeeling. With no prior experience, I've brewed sake in rural Japan cooked a seven-course taster menu in Iceland, and joined a Los Angeles religious cult serving organic vegan food. I've distilled in the town of Tequila and cooked on the Orient Express to Machu Picchu.*
>
> *By the time my project reached its conclusion I had cooked in five of the world's top fifty restaurants.*
>
> *Not bad for a boy who, only a year before, had never stepped inside a professional kitchen.*

Alex later confided in me that one of the biggest takeaways from his whole experience was the 'knock on effect' of connectivity. He would turn up in a country to work in a restaurant for a week, not knowing anybody or anything about that country's food or the restaurant's cooking techniques and with no onward plan.

However, after a few days of connecting with and working alongside chefs in the heat of the kitchen, he was introduced to many different opportunities and avenues through their networks. He would then send out some emails, get his next job offer and then book the next bus, train or plane ticket!

The most incredible thing about Alex's story is that it could be anyone's story. The same principles have worked for us and they can work for you as well, as long as you're willing to put in the effort. There is so much to explore in the world and learn from it. Fortunately, the sharing economy helps even the most common traveller among us establish the connections that make it all possible.

The Reach of Humanity

"You may say I'm a dreamer, but I'm not the only one. I hope someday you'll join us. And the world will live as one."
— John Lennon

During our travels, we have been overwhelmed by the extra effort complete strangers have given to make us feel welcome in their homes. Whilst this is evidenced throughout the book, a quick hotlist will give you a quick glimpse into the wondrous reach of humanity that has been present throughout our journeys.

England, Norfolk Broads - The house was incredible, right on the river. The owner of the house organised a small boat for us to use, free of charge. It was delivered to us on our second morning by the guy who managed the property, he gave us a quick lesson and left us to it. We spent every day out on that little boat and explored the river banks and riverside pubs for miles around.

Canada, Bowen Island, British Columbia - The owner of the house picked us up from Vancouver train station in his brand new eight-seater SUV, he then took us to the local supermarket so we could stock up on supplies. Then he drove us to his home nearby and set the Sat Nav for his holiday home that we would be staying in and left us with the car for ten days. He also invited us to, and paid for lunch, gifted the kids with toys and shared his business contacts so I could network into his circle.

Canada, Muskoka, Ontario - We were landing late into Toronto and that meant we would not arrive to the lakes in Muskoka until around midnight. Our home swap hosts lived in Stratford which was a three-hour drive away. Nonetheless, they insisted on meeting us at the home to welcome us and show us around. They waited until 12:30 a.m. to welcome us, helped us unload and carry the children to bed.

The next morning, they prepared breakfast for us and walked us around the home and property showing us everything we needed to know about the house. They were wonderful people, loved meeting the kids and learning about our travels, and insisted on meeting us again. When we did meet again in their hometown, they gave us a personally guided tour of their business, a furniture making factory that used 100% recycled plastics. It was a great experience and one we all remember fondly.

New Zealand, Lake Tarawera - When I had to be rushed to hospital for an emergency appendectomy, luckily the home swap we had lined up was just forty minutes from the hospital. However, we weren't scheduled to arrive at that particular home swap for another day or two. Once we had explained the situation to the owners of the house, they insisted that we come early at no extra cost in swap points. They also counselled me about the operation as they were both professional medics and offered babysitting services from the friends and neighbours they knew in the area if we should need it.

Australia, Perth, Peppermint Grove Beach - The owner of the house took a three-and-a-half-hour drive to come and make sure we had settled in well and also bought us a Wi-Fi box so that we could connect to emails. He was a lovely guy who had an amazing story, he had been lead Cellist in the John Williams band that played the music for all of your favourite 80s movies, Star Wars, Indiana Jones, Superman, etc.

New Zealand, Carters Beach - I made a huge foul up and filled our car with the wrong fuel. We had to act quick and asked around for mechanics that might be able to help us. We had just left our home swap property after a two week stay and were about to embark on a five-hour drive north. I called the homeowner to ask his advice, only to be offered the house for another week for free! The homeowner then hooked us up with his brother who lived in the town we were in. His brother loaned us the use of his wife's car in an instant and got onto the mechanic to help us with the car.

England, London - Our home swap hosts had stayed to meet us and show us around the house, teach us how the pool and hot tub worked (beginning to get the power of home swapping yet?) and introduce us to their daughter and her family who lived just around the corner who were our point of contact for our stay. They also handed us the car keys and insurance documents as they had kindly arranged for us to use their car whilst we were there and even volunteered to test read this book for me!

Croatia, Vis - We were met at the ferry by the home owner who had already organised a taxi for us. He then followed us back to the house on his moped and insisted he unloaded our luggage. Then he proudly showed us his home and insisted we come and join him and his wife and daughter for lunch at their favourite local restaurant where they also insisted on paying. As this was their second home and lived nearby, they set a date with us for a day that they could come to the house and cook lunch for us! The feast was incredible and throughout the trip they would shower us with invites, wine, food and advice on what to do and see.

South of France - By some random turn of events, we ended up home swapping with a British rock star! He and his wife were wonderful hosts and excellent communicators. They also had a house manager on-site who looked after us perfectly. Throughout our stay, we struck up a great relationship with them via email and have actively stayed in touch. Since then, we have been invited to concerts all over the world and managed to get to Wembley Stadium in London to watch the band play!

France, Dordogne - We used points to arrange a swap in a holiday home in France and arrived into the property for a month long stay where the owners of the house were living just next door. We asked if there were any homeschooling groups nearby that we could join. The owner of the property went one better and told us she could arrange a three-week trial at the local hamlet school. In no time at all, we had met the head teacher and the mayor to discuss and agree to the opportunity, all of which was done in French completely above our understanding level! This resulted in the kids spending three weeks totally immersed in a French school learning the language and culture of France!

In short, just put yourself out there, connect and be open to people, and be amazed at what happens.

TOOLS AND TRICKS

1. Walker, Duncan (Sept 16, 2004) "Live Fast, Die Old", BBC News site. Retrieved 2017-09-4
http://news.bbc.co.uk/1/hi/magazine/3659996.stm

Link to the Ottawa News station YouTube video with Debbie Wosskow about Love Home Swap… can we send it viral?
https://youtu.be/mp-hiBCxpgo

Love Home Swap is the site we used to book over fifty home swaps into over fifteen different countries across three continents.

Here is a special referral link I have organised with the site founders for you to enjoy:
https://www.lovehomeswap.com/princes

www.nomador.com is the site we used to book a house sit for two months in France.

Other sites you can check out are:
www.trustedhousesitter.com
www.housecarers.com
www.homeexchange.com
www.guesttoguest.com
www.airbnb.com
www.vrbo.com
www.rentbyowner.com
www.rentlikeachampion.com

Facebook Groups to check out for swapping and sitting:
House Sitting World

Worldschooler Exchange
Worldschooling Couchsurfing

Other references:
www.carnextdoor.com.au Car sharing in Australia.

www.imoova.com Camper van relocation worldwide.

www.trademe.nz eBay equivalent in New Zealand.

www.blablacar.com is a ride sharing service that connects people who need to travel with drivers who have empty seats.

www.wingly.com is the blabla car of the skies, log in and find out if you can hitch a ride with a pilot!

www.helpx.net Volunteer your services globally for free accommodation.

wwoofinternational.org Volunteer to work on organic farms worldwide in exchange for accommodation

https://www.youtube.com/watch?v=n8UVs_GQ9Ww Totally cringe worthy, self-edited intro from us for the Love Home Swap team.

https://youtu.be/W8Ysp87Po_s Outtakes from said totally cringe worthy self-edited intro for LHS.

https://www.youtube.com/watch?v=pSW3ESAQcMQ Video of how best to search the LHS website.

www.foodishboy.com Alex's personal blog. He is now working at a London-based Foodtech startup called www.citypantry.com. He joined them to lead a team intent on changing the way corporate London views food for their employees. Their goal, bring people together to create a better working environment leading to more fulfilling careers, better engagement, company results and overall happiness. Feel free to reach out to him to learn more!

Chapter 5
Education and World Schooling

"I believe this passionately that we don't grow into creativity, we grow out of it. Or, rather, we get educated out if it."
- Sir Ken Robinson

"Our schools should be ... environments for safe experimentation, viewing failure as an opportunity for learning rather than a mark of shame."
- Salman Khan

"There is no such thing as bad student, only bad teacher."
- Mr. Miyagi

Finally, we got to the front of the queue. It had been another long relocation day. It was mid-afternoon and we had stopped by a supermarket to stock up on supplies. The kids were restless and bored, just like all kids in a supermarket. Clair and I were tired, we just wanted to pack up and pay for the shopping, then get on to our new home for the next few weeks.

The checkout lady said goodbye to the customer in front of us, turned her attention to our family and duly started processing our shopping.

Bleep... Bleep... Bleep... The items moved expertly across the infra-red beam totting up the price as it scuttled down the silver slide waiting for collection at the end.

The checkout lady glanced at Clair and me, then at the kids, then back at us. She pursed her lips, raised an eyebrow, put a slightly condescending tone in her voice and then unleashed the bombshell we had started to get used to… "School holiday today?"

Oh no, not now. I thought. "Ha, no, we are visiting the area."

"School holiday where you come from then?"

Bugger she's not going to let this lie. "Er, no, well, we don't really live anywhere right now. We are travelling."

"Oh. Well, what about the kid's school and their education?"

"We homeschool as we travel."

"Is that allowed?"

"Yes. In fact, it is encouraged in many parts of the world and by many forward-thinking educators."

"But why do you homeschool?" She had that clear look of shock, sorrow, disbelief, outrage and judgement plastered across her face. She pressed on, searching her own thoughts for answers. "Were your children bullied?"

"No, (sigh) we decided to take them out of school and travel the world for as far, wide and as long as we possibly could. We wanted to do as much together as a young family as possible, and now was the right time for us."

This did little to appease her. In fact, she moved to the next level of accusatory interrogation.

"Is that not going to damage their education?"

Jeeeeeez! "No, we don't think so. All of us have already learnt so much as we have travelled. It's been an amazing journey and we feel a much deeper connection to each other and the people we meet."

"But what about the children? How do they socialise? They will never be able to fit back in."

OH GOD! She asked the socialising question!

Here we were, in a new location and on trial by the checkout lady at the local supermarket.

AGAIN!

Luckily, we had become a little numb to the interrogation from complete strangers and actually revelled in some of these confrontations as people unwittingly went through pretty much the exact same form of questioning.

The absolute favourite question — or, for want of a better word, accusation — was that of socialising. It was widely assumed, not to mention highly criticised, that we were damaging our kids' social skills by not exposing them to enough opportunities to be with children their own age.

Don't just take my word for it. Mention that you're thinking of "homeschooling" your children in your next five conversations -- be they with friends, family, co-workers or new acquaintances -- and I guarantee you that all five will bring up the objection that homeschooling would be a detriment to your kids' 'socialising skills.'

Every travelling family we have ever met has cited the same phenomenon. Instant judgement by complete strangers regarding your parental skills and the fact that you are clearly damaging your children by not allowing them to 'socialise'.

Okay. Fine. Let's debunk this myth once and for all. It's ridiculous. Ahem, sorry!

I apologise in advance for the rant, but we've faced this kind of interrogation for years and I really do want to get my point across in a way that comes to me naturally. I am sure there are many well-tailored responses out there from other homeschoolers about the socialising aspect of their children — and I encourage you to read as much as possible on the subject — but for now, this a rawer response!

Apologies aside, let's get back to the myth of homeschooled children being unable to socialise or 'fit in'.

During our travels, we have come in contact with many homeschooled kids and have found them to be the most engaging, confident, easy going, pleasant young people we have ever met. They have this air of confidence that you just don't usually find in children. They are instantly at ease with their surroundings and are able to mingle with anyone in a sensible, engaging and fun way.

They find it second-nature to engage with any human being of any race, colour, culture, nationality, religion, sex, age, height, weight, whatever.

Anyone!

Who wouldn't want that from their kids?

Imagine a world where this tolerance, acceptance and

ability to connect was evident in us all.

Wherever we have been, we have been inundated with praise from people who have met our children and we naturally feel a huge sense of pride when people tell us, "Your kids really are a credit to you!" It makes all the stress and sleepless nights we had when making the decision to travel melt away.

I do, however, want to make a pertinent point about our parenting: Don't, for one second, think that I am trying to paint a picture of 'Butter wouldn't melt in their mouths'.

Hells no.

We, of course, have our moments, struggles, stresses, worries and challenges just like every parent does. We worry hugely about spelling, math, unacceptable behaviour, lack of confidence, connectivity, being driven to the brink of sanity and everything else that goes in-between with raising a family.

What is rather perplexing to us is that we now have to defend all of that -- whereas before, when we were conventionally schooling our children, we didn't. We were part of the status quo then and deemed 'okay' by society at large. Yet, many children in this group are far from perfect in any way, shape or form, but avoid judgement, confrontation or justification for their actions.

Sadly, I think it will always be a case of people judging us by our initial decision, rather than by the results. Which is a huge shame because the results have been nothing short of spectacular and something we truly wish everybody could experience.

Defining Socialisation

"Whenever you find yourself on the side of the majority, it is time to pause and reflect."
- Mark Twain

Since it is the biggest stigma around the subject of homeschooling that we and many other homeschoolers encounter, let's delve a little deeper into this issue of socialisation.

By looking at the definition of the word 'socialise' (or 'socialize', which is a whole other argument), you get the following definitions.

Verb.

1. Mix socially with others.

2. Make someone behave in a way that is acceptable to their society.

What definition, then, are people commonly referring to? Personally, I believe most are generalising and opting for definition one, so let's look at it first.

1. Mix socially with others.

Most people believe that by not going to school our kids are missing out because they are not mixing socially with their peers.
Seriously?
During our travels, we meet new people every day -- on the beach, in a playground, at an ice rink, in the street, on trains, buses and planes, in a restaurant and in hundreds of other places. And guess what, we talked to them. We 'socialised'. Our kids played with their kids. Kids of any age!
It's not like we were sitting inside all day starving them of outside interaction. Of course not. What total nonsense!
Even traditionally homeschooled children who stay at home in one place still have a huge friend base. They meet people at sports, dance, karate, swimming or whatever clubs and interests drive them out into the big scary world of being social.
One could actually argue quite strongly on the flip side of the debate and point to the fact that school is actually anything but 'social'.
How can you call it being 'social' when you are thrust into a classroom with thirty other people and told to sit down, shut up, open your books, do as I do and speak only when spoken to?

Recreation times could barely be called social either. The bulk of this time is generally spent avoiding the people you don't want to see, rather than engaging with as many people as possible in conversation. Barely two weeks into your school life you are niched, packaged, stamped and processed into a subset clique from which you will NEVER be able to escape. Furthermore, you aren't even allowed to approach other groups perceived to be above or below your station!

How is that being social? It's the polar opposite! That can only be described as ANTI-social.

Okay, so with rant number one over, let's look at the second definition.

2. Make someone behave in a way that is acceptable to their society.

Stand up together, sit down together, wear the same clothes together, look the same together, sit at the same desk every day together, don't question authority ever, move when the bell rings, don't run, don't jump, don't play tag, work hard, work harder, rinse and repeat.

Sound familiar?

This is what is acceptable in society and this is what will be accepted in your nine-to-five work existence when you leave school.

This is what we are ultimately teaching children.

Is this the 'socialisation' we have cruelly taken away from our children for a few years? If so, then great!

The underlying issue is this: we collectively forget that we have a choice. We all have the power to change something if it's not working or suiting our child's needs.

What ultimately stands in our way of creating our own happiness is the conventional thinking of the masses. The so-called wisdom of our peers and elders. It is utterly crippling and makes us fear stepping out of line and being perceived as doing something weird or irresponsible.

This fear keeps us in line with the rest of society. 'Socialised.'

So no, you cannot convince me that homeschooling damages your child's ability to socialise.

I encourage you to do your own research on the topic and read as many articles as you can. One article from The Independent in the UK presents the statistics from a study examining homeschoolers' socialisation skills:

> 'Recent data collected by the Department of Education reveals homeschooling has grown by 61.8% over the last ten years to the point where two million kids — 4% of the total youth population — now learn from the comfort of their own home.
>
> Contrary to the belief that homeschooling produces anti-social outcasts, the truth is that some of the most high-achieving, well-adjusted students are poring over math problems at their kitchen table, not a desk in a classroom. According to leading pedagogical research, at-home instruction may just be the most relevant, responsible, and effective way to educate children in the 21st century.'[1]

Focus on Functionality

> "Knowledge which is acquired under compulsion has no hold on the mind. Therefore, do not use compulsion, but let early education be a sort of amusement; you will then be better able to discover the child's natural bent."
> - Plato

Here is another salient point on this debate: Isn't it extraordinary that the people who denounce homeschooling are the people who have never actually homeschooled? What, then, gives them the actionable knowledge to make such sweeping assumptions about your child and your parenting abilities, choices, options or decisions?

When you have the masses on your side, it's easy to criticise those who stand just slightly away from the crowd. This has always been the same throughout human existence, be it racially, sexually, artistically, politically and so on.

As of today, the vast majority of children are

conventionally educated and their parents feel that they have done exactly what they needed to do to ensure that their kids get the best education possible. They have likely made their own sacrifices and life choices to suit that particular child's need.

That is excellent, that is what parenting is all about; but I bet some parents reading this book are still criticised for choosing a particular area or school over another. The judgment extends far beyond the decision to homeschool and into every educational decision parents make. So, ignore the judgment and focus on what works for your family.

Please note that we have actually lived on both sides of this coin and can talk with a clear and balanced perspective about the various educational methods and options available to families. We have schooled our children across Montessori, public, and private schooling institutions. It was our choice to make a change, to action a plan and to take matters into our own hands for a while. Homeschooling, world schooling, online schooling — call it what you will — it is still schooling.

The bottom line is that individuals are learning.
I am of the absolute conviction that there is a place for all of the above methods of tuition, yet there is no perfect one. Every person is different, every school is different, every teacher is different and every situation is different.

In the end, it's not so much about the method of choice but the end goal. It's not that we are staunchly against the education system. No, not at all. Nor are we staunchly for the homeschooling or world schooling movement. We totally believe that there is room for both and fully understand that each family's needs are and always will be completely different to those of others.

What does need to change is the stigma that surrounds an alternative approach to education. We each need the freedom from social pressures to adjust to our unique situations providing us the ability to make the correct decisions for our families and the individual needs of our children.

Give It a Trial Run

Still, as radical as it sounds, I personally believe that every family should homeschool or world school for at least one or two years as their circumstances permit. In her definitive guide to world schooling, author Ashley Dymock de Tello summarises exactly why it's worth giving world schooling at least a trial run:

> Why choose world schooling over the other options available to you? In part, because you don't really have to choose it over something else. Instead, world schooling is a tool available to enhance whatever educational approach you choose to take
>
> World schooling [works because it] demands greater participation from the child. Whether you combine world schooling with homeschooling, unschooling, or some type of formal or alternative schooling, a child who travels cannot avoid the opportunities to learn.
>
> Learning becomes a survival skill when you are far outside your comfort zone. And, for most of us, travel has a way of pushing us well beyond our comfort zones. The same is true for children. Providing a child with new cultures, countries, peoples and environments from which to learn is one of the best ways to jumpstart their natural instinct to learn. Even if you cannot see it happening, they are absorbing so much more than airplane rides or camping trips.
>
> Because of this, world schooling works on an entirely different level because it not only demands and inspires greater participation from the child, but it also forces the parent to allow for more student-paced, self-directed learning.

In addition, as a father, homeschooling allowed me a much closer view of my children's educational development. I knew what they were learning and could be an active agent in their learning process. And all of this was possible whilst still allowing for each child's self-directed learning.

This process not only gives you such a different view of your children but also gives you a much greater appreciation for the teachers that you will come into contact with if you ever decide to return to the conventional school system.

For example, we have now learned exactly how each of our children learn: what inspires them, what bores them, how they respond to certain things, what mental blocks they have and how best to adjust our course when tutoring them.

Finding this out was a hell of a journey, especially with our twins. One would expect them to be quite similar in many respects, but nothing could be farther from the truth. Their learning styles and work ethic are, in fact, polar opposites. This led to huge frustration for us and, of course, for them too.

However, now that we have been through that learning process ourselves, we can empathise and fully understand the teacher's insights when sitting through parent evenings, reviews and appraisals.

Instead of us sitting there thinking, No way is our little girl like that! She must have been misunderstood or misguided by a troublesome peer, now we generally stop the teacher mid-sentence and say, "WE KNOW, IT DRIVES US NUTS, TOO!"

This breaks down the wall and we can then have a level-headed and oftentimes amusing conversation about what to do, the best course of action and how we as parents can help at home to make life a little easier for the teacher.

(To add a little more spice to these parent evenings, we are currently having these conversations in French -- or, for want of a better term, Franglais!)

The Misconception

"Just when you think you know something, you have to look at in another way. Even though it may seem silly or wrong, you must try."
- John Keating aka O Captain My Captain

The biggest misconception about homeschooling is that people generally think of a situation where conventional school is moved to the home. People envision desks in the lounge and fixed times with a timetable for Math, English, Science, lunch break, play break, etc.

They also fear they are not qualified or 'clever enough' to teach their own children and are doing them an injustice. Homeschooling just doesn't work that way. You can teach your own kids. You are already doing it all the time without knowing.

Everybody homeschools!

You teach manners, play games, make crafts, build Lego, cook, play football, walk, skate, run, take pictures, play instruments, help with homework, read books, etc. Whatever it is you do together, it is all teaching.

Anything you don't know how to teach can be learnt from the internet in a matter of minutes.

You can also reward your child for their efforts too. Recently, our son was in a swimming pool when he suddenly decided that he wanted to see how many lengths he could swim before he got tired. I watched, amazed, as he smashed out ten lengths. I then paced out the pool and told him he had just swam 100 metres!

He was chuffed with his efforts and I was astounded that he had just decided to do this himself, no pressures, no swim club, no trainer and no dangled carrot, just his own internal desire. In most cases, kids get a badge or certificate for this kind of effort, but there was no 'official' person there to verify it and I felt pretty bad that he wouldn't get an opportunity to share his achievement.

Then it dawned on me that I had seen it: I had counted the laps, I had encouraged him, and if I wanted to reward him with a certificate then damn it I would. We didn't need some bored P.E. teacher waltzing up and down the side of the pool in a pair of ill-fitting Speedos with a clicker in one hand, stop watch in the other and a whistle around their neck.

It took fifteen seconds to find a swimming certificate online, print it off, write in his name and his achievement, date and sign it. He proudly posed with his certificate so that a picture could be sent to his grandparents and he now has it displayed above his bed. That act alone has inspired him to swim further and he has randomly chosen sixteen lengths to shoot for next time!

Don't fear that you are not qualified to teach your child. Do we honestly think your child's primary school teacher is capable of reciting the periodic table? No, they don't have to. So why, then, do us parents put the fear of God into ourselves and hide behind the 'I am not smart enough to teach my children' excuse?

We have all grown up in a society that has made us believe that the teacher is all knowing, all powerful and always correct. But, as many teachers will tell you, that's just not the case.

Some might argue that many teachers in the education system now are those who have fallen into teaching jobs. It is rare to find those who have a true vocation for it. And even if they do have that calling and are wonderful teachers, there will still be a certain percentage of the class that they just won't and can't connect with. It's unfair to expect otherwise. There is no magic wand to wave over thirty people and have them all understand the method and the subject in which they are being taught.

What's more, even a history teacher who has just left University with a teaching and History degree focusing on Victorian England must go through the same learning process you would in order to teach most any subject.

For example, upon walking into their new job, the history teacher in question may be told that the syllabus for next year is the American Civil War. They will now have to hit the internet and books to learn about the subject to be able to teach it. That is the same playing field as the homeschooling parent.

If you need a real-life example, a few years ago I wrote a blog about education and homeschooling that contains a little anecdote that further cements the point I am trying to convey about our role as parents in our children's education.

> We have been travelling nonstop now for seven months since originally writing this tab in the blog, which seems to have whizzed by! Of course, the heaviest baggage that we carry around with us from port to port is the worry of our kid's education. No matter what we tell ourselves, or how much we have seen the kids engaged in their surroundings having fun and learning at the same time, the nagging doubt over

this subject and of social pressure/compliance or whatever you want to label it, is a constant drag on our parental subconscious. We have to constantly remind ourselves of the reasons that compelled us to take this trip in the first place, but sometimes the reasons are offered up on a platter!

For example. Whilst sitting in on a rainy day in Switzerland helping Sophia with some English problems, we came across this little gem in the English activity book that we had kept from her school to travel with.

(The task was to choose a fitting word with which to fill in the blank and spell it correctly.)

Spelling 1.

1. That is such a _____ elephant. It must have weigh tons of kilogram.

Laughable at best. Disgraceful, of course. But pause and think about this. Think about how she would have HAD to fill in this blank with something, anything, because leaving it blank would have resulted in the dreaded Red Cross, crippling her confidence and self-motivation. It's 'anti-teaching'.

Reflecting on this post again today just reconfirms to me the unwavering knowledge that I can give my children a better education than that. Don't doubt yourself. My wife and I have learnt far more from homeschooling and travelling than we ever did at school! We trust that our children will too.

The Freedom of Flexibility

"I never teach my pupils, I only provide the conditions in which they can learn."
- Albert Einstein

It's also worth noting that it doesn't have to be forever. You have the choice to do whatever suits you best. If you feel homeschooling isn't working, then look back into the schooling route again, perhaps even a Montessori school or other educational groups in your area. In our case, and even though they can't speak the language, our kids are enjoying being in a school environment again, for now.

After two-and-a-half years of constant travel we felt the pull to sit still for a while and the kids had shown an interest in going to school again. This was quite a strange position to be in when you have four kids who actually want to go to school.

My wife and I asked ourselves, 'If we could give our kids the perfect life gift, what would it be?'

Our overwhelming answer was for them to have the ability to speak another language, and that is something that sadly we cannot teach them ourselves. So, we asked the kids, "What country have you really enjoyed and what language would you like to learn?" Luckily for us, they all said France and French!

With a clear goal ahead of us, we got to looking into the possibility of long term house sits, home swaps or rental options. In the end, we managed to arrange a good property rental deal with a fellow Love Home Swap member that suited both our needs.

As for the schooling, the kids have fit in really well, even though they walked in with zero knowledge of French. Being back in a system again is quite strange, the youngest three are in a primary school which is leaning towards a Montessori style of teaching and is proving to be an awesome experience. Our eldest daughter is in the equivalent to UK Senior School and has blossomed into a young adult. Her language skills have shone as she has pushed herself to communicate and make friends with her peers.

It is a very strange experience for my wife and me who were suddenly left alone all day in what seemed to be complete silence. We also struggle of course with stepping back into a system again.

Our approach towards schooling and one we have to keep drilling into the kids is to not worry about any evaluations, tests or difficulties with certain subjects. We tell them we don't care if test scores are low and if they aren't connecting with a certain subject. We can always study that at our own pace at home or in a different environment another day.

What is the most important thing for them is that they get to learn the language and speak it naturally, and thankfully that will be achieved through total immersion and play. The language and the experience are the goal, nothing else. Anything more that they might achieve is great, we would have found another natural talent or interest in each of them.

We are using the educational system to suit our own needs. Now that we've completed our first school year in France, we will monitor how it has gone and adjust course again if and when need be.

Some will criticise the randomness and 'unsettling' nature of this approach. Of course, we will have to contend with many doubters. But, as always, we usually underestimate too quickly how adaptable we all are, especially children. Besides, isn't variety the spice of life?

It is obviously a hard decision to make when it comes to your child's education. Naturally, we all want the absolute best for them.

The only advice I can offer is that you do not get caught up in nonsense arguments about how one choice or the other will hurt you child's ability to socialise. Or worse, listen to advice from people who have never actually homeschooled or educated their children alternatively in any way before.

Try and find out as much as you can about alternative ways to educate and keep an open mind to trying them out. When you give your children the flexibility to learn how and where they learn best, you remove so much of the rubbish that weighs down the conventional education system and gift them the freedom to learn.

"The tragedy is that society (your school, your boss, your government, your family) keeps drumming the genius part out. The problem is that our culture has engaged in a Faustian bargain, in which we trade our genius and artistry for apparent stability."
- Seth Godin

More Than a Theory

Now, I am sure you are wondering 'Hey, yeah, that's all cool, but how did you homeschool whilst travelling? What was your day-to-day schedule like? How did you structure learning and engage your kids?"

Ah, well, all very good questions. I have to be very careful here not to paint a picture of serenity wherein all the children sat at their desks, back's straight, big smiles, perfect manners, inquisitive questions and total attention.

That never ever happened! But, I think it's safe to say that doesn't happen in a school environment either! The way we structured it was different in every location and slowly progressed over time.

When we first left for the trip, we were still wary of the fact that we were doing something very strange. It had been a big decision and we knew we had better take it extremely seriously. We had huge anxieties over the education of the children and we were all too cognisant of the social pressures we were putting on ourselves and the kids.

In retrospect, we probably went at it a little too hard in the early days. We tried doing some math, reading, spelling and some kind of art or science project every day and to have some set times. This was naturally met with a huge push back from the kids, which was then met with huge disdain from the parents, which would end up in a huge mess of emotions!

We soon learnt that each child would have a different time of day when you could sense they would be more responsive. It could be a simple question, or a moment of boredom that could open them up to sitting with you and reading or doing a math puzzle or crossword. This would then lead into a spelling test or breaking out a math book that we travelled with to test or learn new skills.

Here is a working example for you: My oldest daughter (then eight) walked into the room one day and saw me writing the blog. She started to ask questions about how I was building the website and how I had taught myself to build websites in the first place. This was a classic golden opportunity to engage in her curiosity and turn it into a lesson about website design and uploading content. In fact, this particular example went even deeper and prompted her to launch her own website and business, which was a pancake delivery service around our neighbours' houses.

Out of that project we covered basic math, website creation, content creation, marketing, customer engagement, cooking, sourcing ingredients and door-to-door sales techniques.

She also printed out flyers and employed the family members into the business! You can check it out at
www.princepancakedelivery.weebly.com.

Was it a successful business? Hell no! Only two orders! But that was just another lesson about rejection and target markets. However, the smile that the two orders put on the kids' faces was worth all the effort!

Another day we bought a huge drum of distilled water as it was much cheaper to buy in bulk and better for the environment than buying individual bottles. Drinking tap water in Koh Samui is a big no, no!

We got the water home, only to realise that it was impossible for me to hold it long enough (I am no Arnie!) to put into smaller bottles that we could store in the fridge. This problem then turned into a science project for the kids to learn about siphons and the movement of water.

We hit the internet and started the research, looking into the explanations of how and why it worked. Once we had sourced the materials and put the plan into action, they were thrilled to see it work and had no idea they had been learning math and science along the way.

When we visited cities, it was much easier to conduct lessons as the city itself was the classroom. When we were in Rome, we had booked a slot to visit the Colosseum. Before we went out that day, we watched a few YouTube clips of the movie Gladiator and other free film content, including a history programme. After that, they were hooked and couldn't wait to go see this fascinating stadium where the gladiators had fought both each other and wild animals to the death.

Once we had the buy-in from the kids, we could then layer on other facts as the day unfolded. We talked about the year the Colosseum was built (construction started in 70 AD!), the architecture, and the huge strain and effort it took for the thousands of slaves who were forced to work on it and died whilst building it. We also discussed the emperors of the time and the history of the games and the shows that took place there.

Instead of a one-hour history lesson looking at books and not engaging with the topic at all, the kids found themselves completely immersed in a learning experience without really knowing it that lasted a full day. They were just having fun.

It's important to note that this didn't happen all of the time. Life was not a dreamy walk around a city pointing at interesting facts and getting nods and smiles. There were dozens of times (maybe more) where we would get huge resistance from the kids. They didn't want to go out that day, or they just couldn't walk into another church, cathedral, castle or temple. They were too tired to walk another two kilometres to get back to the car or train station and were just fed up and tired and wanted to eat ice cream and go home.

Life is not a bed of roses. However, we were together and we were pushing the boundaries of living the life that we wanted to lead, and that was ultimately what mattered. The fact that deep learning could happen whilst we were pursuing that life is what made world schooling such a valuable tool for our family travels. It was adaptable to every circumstance and helped us realise that learning can happen anywhere and in many unconventional ways.

World schooling will look and feel different for every family — and it will likely change over time within each family, as well. That's the beauty of it. You can mold and shape it to fit your child's needs and your family's travel circumstances. That adaptability and personalization of education is something your children would never receive from the one-size-fits-all approach of traditional

- - - - - - - - - - -

Thoughts From Clair

Originally, when Dan mentioned taking a while to go

travelling with the kids, I was both excited and afraid. I knew that life in Singapore was coming to an end and that we needed to make a change. We talked and talked about our fears for the kids, their schooling and what would happen if we were to throw away everything that we had worked so hard to build up.

I spoke with a couple of our friends who are well respected international school teachers, and to my surprise they thought that world schooling was a brilliant idea. I was given thoughts and tips for the kids' education, and gained a bit of confidence that our children would be okay. Besides, they were still so young (the twins were only three and wouldn't need formal education for a few years).

When we told our friends our thoughts and ideas, some of them thought that we were crazy and met our announcements with blank stares and criticism. Others thought that it was a great idea to travel with the kids and wished that they were brave enough to do it too.

For the first month after we left Singapore, our new life felt just like a holiday. Of course, we missed our friends greatly, but it all still felt temporary. After a while, we got into our routines. I was surprised to realise that Dan was better at the homeschooling than I was. I had, of course, been the one who spent many hours trying to help the kids with their homework and practicing reading during our old life and I presumed that I would continue doing most of the school work with the kids when we weren't out exploring or learning from excursions. It was a pleasant surprise to find out this wouldn't be the case.

At first, Dan and I felt a fair bit of pressure to school our children (pressure that we mostly put on ourselves due to the fact that we were still questioning whether taking the kids out of school was a good idea or not). We questioned (or had other people question) our decision to homeschool for a long, long part of our travels. Now that the kids are studying in French schools, we still continue to question this route too. I think that when you have more than one option, it's just human nature.

However, perhaps due to the pressure that we had put on ourselves – and the fact that I was trying to teach four children different things – I would often get quite frustrated with the kids lack of enthusiasm or concentration. Dan had much more patience (which surprised all of us, himself included) for tutoring.

After speaking with other world schooling parents for advice, they smiled and said that they had been there too. The advice was to take the pressure off, take it off of ourselves and off the kids too. They pointed out that the kids were learning so much every day with the travels and to trust in their own interests and intuition.

Interestingly enough, by taking the pressure off our second daughter (who was struggling to learn to read) she achieved a huge breakthrough. One day, she picked up the first Harry Potter book and started reading it in her head. And then the next book and the next. Now, she may have been making mistakes and missing parts of the story-line, but she was reading. And, most importantly, she was enjoying it!

Please, do not think for one minute that taking your children out of school to travel short- or long-term will ever hold them back in their education or life. It will do the opposite. They will flourish. I have seen it with my own kids and with many other travelling children. In many cases, returning children start achieving grades far higher than they ever had before and shine a light far brighter than they could have ever thought possible.

From personal experience, we have seen our oldest daughter transition from world schooling to traditional French schooling with ease. She has enjoyed wonderful experiences, loved every minute of it, made a ton of new friends, gone on numerous school trips (including a one week camping holiday), and is all but fluent in French.

She can't wait for the summer holidays to be over so she can get back to school. We hope that feeling lasts, but if it doesn't for some reason, then we know we have options. We are not afraid to start looking around for alternatives because we now have the confidence, knowledge, and power to change the situation if we need to. For us, that is the true power of world schooling.

But don't just take it from me, let's ask my oldest daughter Kaitlyn her thoughts!

Thoughts From A Worldschooler

Enter Kaitlyn (twelve) -

What did you like and dislike about home and world schooling?

I loved homeschooling because you could learn about whatever you want and you could do whatever you want and not be stuck in a classroom listening to a teacher jabber on that goes through your ears and out the other side. We also went to historic places and learned about facts that you wouldn't know in a classroom. It was really cool going to historic places like that.

The thing I disliked about homeschooling and travelling was I had to leave my friends behind. That was fine after a little while because we kept in touch with Skype and email. And when we travelled to a place and stayed for a week or two we would make new friends. That was great meeting new people, but sad knowing there's a chance we'll never see them again. But now I go to school and I'm moving on to my second year at this school and I love it. Of course I didn't like being forced to sit in front of books and practice maths and english, but homeschooling was really nice and a break from life. I really enjoyed it.

How did your first day at a French school make you feel, considering you hadn't been to school for over two years and didn't even speak the language?

I was very nervous and I had butterflies in my stomach, but the second I got there I met a very nice English girl who helped me.

Unfortunately, we weren't put into the same class, but I met another amazing French girl who helped me, even though she doesn't speak English! She is my best friend to this day. She helped me so much on the first day and I didn't feel nervous anymore. Whenever I'm with her I don't feel nervous. After a week or two, I had a big group of friends who I loved, laughed, and hung out with, and the French were so kind and helpful and understood I couldn't speak the language. The teachers were very nice and explained things in English for me and after a couple of months I was getting the hang of it so I didn't really need their help anymore. I love all my teachers and they are very kind and funny.

I am very happy because I have good grades even though I am not quite fluent in French. I take the bus every morning at 7 a.m. from a town just a five-minute drive from our house. It takes forty to fifty minutes to get to my school, which at first I was nervous about because it was so far away (and I wasn't very comfortable sitting on a bus with just French people), but now I love it. I sit there listening to my music looking at the castles and rivers, or I try and get some extra sleep!

TOOLS AND TRICKS

1. To read the whole report in the independent about homeschooling you can find it at:
http://www.independent.co.uk/life-style/homeschooling-smartest-way-to-teach-kids-a7652796.html

2. Probably the best and most recent book on the subject of world schooling is written by Ashley Dymock de Tello, *World Schooling: How to Revolutionize Your Child's Education Through Travel*
https://www.amazon.com/World-Schooling-Revolutionize-Education-Through-ebook/dp/B06XWJBQXY/

When researching the topic of education, we found Sir Ken Robinson's TED talk titled 'Do Schools Kill Creativity.' At 47 million views, it is the most popular TED talk of all time, signalling a huge interest in the change of how we look and think about education.

https://www.ted.com/talks/ken_robinson_says_schools_kill_creativity

Sir Ken has more talks on the subject which can be found here:
https://www.ted.com/talks/ken_robinson_changing_education_paradigms
https://www.ted.com/talks/ken_robinson_how_to_escape_education_s_death_valley
https://www.ted.com/talks/sir_ken_robinson_bring_on_the_revolution

The link to our homeschooling tab, which includes many TED talks and other inspiring videos about education from speakers such as Sal Khan, Seth Godin and Prince Ea.
http://princesoffthegrid.weebly.com/homeschooling.html

www.khanacademy.org is, in my opinion, the best online teaching tool we have ever used for multiple subjects in one place. It includes Science, Math, Grammar, Coding, History and much more. Sal Khan, the founder of Khan Academy delivers one of my favourite TED talks ever:
https://www.ted.com/talks/salman_khan_let_s_use_video_to_reinvent_education

www.noredink.com is an excellent website for learning grammar.

www.sumdog.com is great for teaching basic math to young kids.

Squeebles is an app for teaching kids multiplication tables.

www.studyladder.com for online learning fun

www.code.org for learning how to code.

www.readingeggs.com.au/apps - an app to help your child learn to read

Language learning apps include: Duolingo, Memrise and Reverso

Montessori style teaching is explained in depth here on Wiki https://en.wikipedia.org/wiki/Montessori_education

Our friend Sarah Etherington is an online Montessori teacher who would be happy to connect with anybody looking to learn more! http://sarahetherington.wixsite.com/lolgreenglobal

Watch me eat fried insects in a Thai market for a world school project. https://youtu.be/xL6z00zZJUw

Facebook group - If you would like further information, validation or want to connect with many world schoolers, there is a Facebook group called "Worldschoolers" which has almost 30,000 members from people all over the world.

Reach out and say hi!

Chapter 6
Finances and Accounting

> "It is not the man who has too little, but the man who craves more, that is poor."
> - Seneca

    The podcast interview was going pretty well, my nerves had subsided and the host was really interested in how we had managed to home swap our way around the world. My fears of being grilled about our lifestyle had abated and we were into a great flow chatting back and forth in a comfortable manner.

    Then he hit me with it, "How can you afford to live like this? You must be some kind of millionaire!"

    Gulp, the dreaded money question. It's what people always want to know and, of course, he had to ask it -- if not for himself and his own knowledge, certainly for his listeners!

    Well, do you want to know the crazy truth? It's cheaper to travel than to actually sit still in normal everyday life. After two and a half years of non-stop travel, we needed a rest and hired a house in France for nine months. We were shocked to realise that we were spending in one month what we would have generally spent in three months when on the road.

    Just from settling down, we have added the expenses of rent, electricity, water, telecom bills, school, clothes for four children in four seasons, school books, school lunches, school trips and other activities to pay for on top of the fuel (depending on where we swapped), and food bills that we would always have paid when travelling.

    For now, we will dip into savings. That's what they are for!

It's important to stress that you don't have to be rich to travel. That is a complete fallacy. Stop and ponder how dreadlocked hippie eighteen-year-old students can afford it and you can't!? Think about the single mom that is travelling the world with her two children versus the billionaire CEO who is divorced twice, never sees his kids and doesn't have enough time to take a week off for a holiday, let alone six months to one year. Who is richer in that scenario?

Sure, you might not be staying in the usual five-star hotel rooms you have become accustomed to over the last few years, but you aren't looking to. As outlined in the earlier home swapping chapter, you can actually get accommodation for free. And if you can drive to that location then you are potentially saving a ton of cash on flights too.

If you own your home and have the mortgage to pay, arranging long-term home swaps is an option, but that won't cover your mortgage costs. If you don't want to home swap but still want to travel long term, you can look at renting your apartment or house out whilst you are gone. The monthly rental will cover your mortgage costs and likely even cover stays in an Airbnb-listed property with cash to spare for food and sightseeing.

In fact, we met one American family that did exactly this and it worked out brilliantly for them. They had found good tenants and were safe in the knowledge that their home was being looked after whilst they were away for the year. The money they made from the rent kept them travelling far longer and further than they could ever have imagined.

Note also that your home country currency will probably go a very long way in other countries. Asia is especially cheap in places such as Thailand, Vietnam and Cambodia. Parts of Europe can be expensive, but others are considered extremely cheap. In Southern Spain, you can get beers and Tapas for one euro! Croatia is also an inexpensive place to visit and the friendliness of the locals is incredible.

Many travelling families we have met love other European countries such as Romania and Bulgaria, however most wax lyrical about South American countries as they are so unspoilt with an abundance of natural beauty and are dirt cheap to live and travel within!

Remember, you need to break your mindset from those five grand holidays you take every year in that same all-inclusive resort. That is not your goal here!

We got into the habit of keeping a spreadsheet wherever we went and tried to fill it in every day with what we had spent. Our goal each day was to spend nothing. Ridiculous, huh? Well, not really once we started to get the hang of it. If we had already done a supermarket shop, what else could we possibly need?

For example, in the cities where we stayed, we could always walk to parks or tourist sites with free admission such as museums, churches, cathedrals, gardens, etc. If you pack a picnic and some snacks with a bottle of water, you needn't spend a penny all day. You can always get the bottle refilled at water fountains or restaurants, bars, hotels or coffee shops. Just ask, people love to help!

We also found that, on the flip side, once that first penny leaves your pocket you are psychologically screwed and they start flowing out. Buy a coffee, then an ice cream, then a sandwich, then a postcard, then whatever it is that your mind has suddenly decided you absolutely must have and somehow end up buying!

We found that by filling a great big juicy fat zero into the spreadsheet at the end of our day it set our minds up perfectly for the next day's challenge of another 'Zero Dollar Day'. Our best ever streak was four straight days, not one single penny spent, but still having an unbelievable time and seeing as much as we could of wherever we were.

As an example, I will share with you how much we spent for one month in Southern Spain. Naturally, accommodation was free as we were home swapping, but our total bill for that whole month still racked up to be €2712.

I chose this particular month as an example because I wanted to give you an idea of how it seems like a lot, until you realise what we managed to achieve during that time.

What is important to remember here is that, of course, we are a large family and we all like our food. Feeding six people is always going to be our biggest concern and expense, and the above total includes weekly shops in the local market or supermarkets.

We had also hired a car for the whole month, so included in the aforementioned total is the cost of the hire itself, plus the fuel and various parking fees too.

During the month, we visited Ronda, Gibraltar, Malaga, Marbella, Puerto Banus, Nerja and many of the tiny beautiful Spanish villages and towns. We also visited friends in Seville for the Semana Santa festival during Easter and drove to Granada to visit the Alhambra palace.

However, what the numbers don't tell is that during this month we celebrated our wedding anniversary at a lovely restaurant. We also had the small matter of celebrating Clair's 40th birthday in style and hosted her parents over four days.

Still included in the total mentioned above was the privately chartered crewed yacht that sailed us around the Mediterranean from Marbella, a surprise spa visit, lunch and another wonderful dinner for the whole family.

With all of that in mind, does it not actually seem rather cheap?

There is no one magic budget for you to follow or for me to advise you on. Each individual's situation is completely different to the next. It is going to depend a lot on where you are travelling and how you are getting there, how long you will stay, and what you want to achieve there.

If you are going to Southeast Asia to rent a beach bungalow, eat fruit for five days a week and fast for the other two, then you will spend very little. However, if you are travelling through New Zealand and want to go whale watching, jet boating, skiing, take a helicopter to a glacier and visit the Milford and Doubtful Sounds, then it's going to be expensive!

Naturally, some costs you can't avoid. With growing children, we can side-step most clothing costs in the form of hand me downs, but if the eldest is growing out of shoes and clothes then she needs some new ones. But again, this can all be bought relatively cheaply nowadays with supermarket clothing or cheaper line brands. Or, even better, you can find great deals by dropping into the local charity shops. We once bought a jumper for fifty pence in England as the weather turned a little colder!

The underlying message is that, ultimately, if you really

do want to break free and take a work sabbatical, money is not your enemy. It will not and should not hold you back. You can make it work, it just takes a little planning and a tiny amount of discipline. You will be shocked how little you can actually live on.

"But Won't You Go Bankrupt and end up living under a bridge?" Yes, we do get asked this kind of question and of course it was one of those big awful self-imposed fears that we faced during our decision-making process.

In retrospect, I can't believe we actually ever feared this. It's complete nonsense. The way we got over this fear was again to ask ourselves, 'If that actually happened, what would we do to fix it?'

As I established in my fear setting exercise, the answer would be to live with family for six months or so until we got ourselves back on our feet. Nobody is unemployable, nobody is incapable of making money and nobody should ever fear having to live with the few people in the world that truly love and want the best for you.

If living with family in a warm house being fed three times a day with clothes on our backs, the use of the internet, car, TV and running hot and cold water was a worst-case scenario, why on earth were we fearing it?

How Do I Make Money?

> "I can live without money, but I cannot live without love."
> - Judy Garland

Another commonly asked question that follows the 'you don't have to be a millionaire" response is, "So ... how do you make money?"

Good question.

My initial goal when we left to start travelling was to create some kind of business that I could run from a laptop from anywhere in the world. Ahem, that is still my goal, although at time of writing I have just accepted my first paying customers for my advisory and mentor services to two startup companies based in London.

What I found once we started travelling was that the bulk of the day was completely taken up with sightseeing, schooling, preparing meals, travelling or tending to administrative tasks such as banking, researching home swaps, target destinations, flights, writing the blog, car hire, etc. etc., so for me it was an unrealistic goal to think I could just launch some kind of business from a laptop.

That being said, I have met many people who have managed to start their online business and get inspiration from their stories of how they have finally broken completely free from the chains of a company and office job.

There are loads of digital nomads out in this world who are working purely from a laptop and travelling the world at their leisure. There is no reason you couldn't do it either whilst world schooling and travelling. In fact, sometimes opportunities fall inadvertently into your lap. Take, for example, our friend and fellow world schooler Michelle Holmes, a Visibility Mentor to 'World Changing Women' who has helped her clients to generate millions and to serve thousands.

After a series of health complaints, Michelle was introduced to and fell in love with essential oils. She was amazed at their benefit to her, but also appreciated how they affected her whole family and close group of friends.

To her absolute excitement, this new-found interest also presented her with an interesting business opportunity. The best brand of essential oils she could find, and preferred to use, were from a company called doTerra, which chose not to go down the traditional route of getting a product to market (celebrity endorsement and relentless advertising) but instead to grow by word of mouth.

Michelle now educates families on how they too can use essential oils to reduce the number of toxins they are exposed to on a daily basis, live a natural healthy lifestyle, be healthier and happier and if they wish to, build a thriving natural health business that makes a difference in the world and creates financial freedom too!

Michelle's passion for this business is undeniable, and she soon plans to tour the UK with her husband and two children in an RV so she can meet and train her growing UK team whilst seeing new sights, visiting friends and family, meeting new people and world schooling along the way!

Michelle can be found at michelle-holmes.com if you are interested in natural health or building a business around it whilst you world school!

If you are looking for information on how to start your own business and need some validation and confidence, I suggest gathering inspiration and ideas from the following people:

Tim Ferriss: Twitter @tferriss

In his book, *The 4-Hour Workweek*, Ferriss discusses the concept of a 'muse', how to create a low-maintenance business that will arm you with a residual monthly revenue.

> **"Our goal is simple, to create an automated vehicle for generating cash without consuming time."**
> - Tim Ferriss, *The 4-Hour Workweek*

You can find Tim at his blog www.thefourhourworkweek.com where you can listen to his incredible podcast interviews with some of the world's leading icons across many different areas of life by subscribing to The Tim Ferriss show.

Seth Godin: Twitter @thisissethsblog

Seth is an author of several bestselling books, as well as an entrepreneur, marketer, public speaker and creator of awesome courses (which you can check out on Udemy.com). His teaching in creating value and helping you make the distinction between whether or not you are a freelancer or entrepreneur are just two of the invaluable courses he teaches. I have personally downloaded the Value Creation Master Class and found it to be excellent.

He is also the proud founder of the ALT MBA and his daily blog is arguably the best free content on the internet. He commits himself to writing daily posts, and the wisdom he shares is a wonderful daily kick in the butt!

www.sethgodin.com.

Noah Kagan: Twitter @Noahkagan

Noah was employee number thirty at Facebook before going on to founding his own company called **www.appsumo.com**, a website dedicated to getting great deals for entrepreneurs, or as Noah would say, a Groupon for geeks. The site runs daily deals that are hugely beneficial to bloggers, online business owners, entrepreneurs and freelancers of all kinds!

www.Sumo.com is the sister site creating tools, tips and hacks for entrepreneurs to automate site growth.

Noah also designed and offers a course called 'How To Make A 1k Per Month Business', which aims to transfer you from a 'Wantrepreneur to an Entrepreneur'. I have participated in this online course and found it to be hugely insightful. The FB support group for this course is also a great community in which you can ask questions, get support, inspiration and ideas.

You can find the course here https://appsumo.com/how-to-make-your-first-dollar/

Noah and the Appsumo guys are probably the most fun bunch out there and they have a ton of free content on their website and YouTube channel. Make sure you check them out and get to know them. I am sure you will be impressed with what they are doing!

You can also listen to the Noah Kagan Presents podcast to listen to some awesome interviews and get some great insights.

Ramit Sethi: Twitter @Ramit

Ramit is the author of the book, *I Will Teach You To Be Rich* and runs the site and blog of the same name. Ramit has created many different courses that teach people how to take life into their own hands, such as the course on finding your first profitable idea. He explains:

Whether you have no business ideas or too many, discover how to find the ONE profitable idea that will start making you money today.

You can also sign up to Ramit's blog, which he writes and updates himself almost daily. The content is hugely insightful, but best of all it's free!

For more in-depth knowledge of the above people, make sure you check out Tim Ferriss's podcast. Each one of them has been a guest on his show and have shared their huge insights for your free listening pleasure!

Make Wise Investments

Now, please don't think I have tried to dodge the original question of 'How do you make money?'
I have not yet built my passive income from creating a business, but have started consulting for three exciting London-based startup companies. I get great enjoyment from connecting with young and hungry people willing to action advice whilst learning new strategies and techniques to help them, their customers and their employees succeed.
Apart from this, we rely on investments I made before we left and have subsequently made along the way. In fact, by stepping out of my usual surroundings, I have been able to learn about many different areas of business and make some investments that I would never have made if I were still sat at my desk. Take for example a forestry project in France, a Peruvian agricultural firm and cryptocurrencies such as Bitcoin, Ethereum or Dash. Thankfully for us, these investments have paid off and continue to do so.
2020 Update: Since writing this part of the book I have studied Bitcoin and Austrian Economics at great length and now never recommend Ethereum or Dash. Bitcoin is the only worthwhile cryptocurrency and an exciting opportunity

for humanity to reorganise itself on a sound monetary and economic structure. I have even started a Bitcoin-focused podcast and interview people from all over the world about this subject. I hope you get the time to check out a few episodes. https://anchor.fm/daniel-prince6"

There is no magic wand to wave here or timely stock tip or macro market advice to impart. All I can really advise is that you should always try to look into investment opportunities that give you some kind of edge over the masses — or, as Warren Buffet would advise, do the opposite to the crowd.

Many books have been written about this subject. Many are terrible; however, some are truly astonishing and give you a much better understanding of the economy and how you can grow your capital and make your money work for you so that you can step off the gas!

What's more, thanks to the age of technology that we live in, independent broadcasting companies are coming to the fore to provide us with real insights instead of the usual rubbish you find on mainstream news and business channels.

If you are interested in learning from some of the greats, you should check out the following:

www.realvisiontv.com this site was founded by financial market veterans Grant Williams and Raoul Pal. They made it their mission to fly around the world and interview the world's most incredible economic minds.

I have profited personally from learning about a vast array of different markets and investment ideas that have been portrayed in the interviews and couldn't thank the founders enough!

The videos are of brilliant quality and the insights will blow you away. Even market veterans will find these interviews to be completely captivating. Check out their free trial, you will be amazed.

You can also subscribe to their podcast on iTunes called *Adventures In Finance*. This is, again, a completely free education.

One Up On Wall Street by Peter Lynch was the first book about the financial markets that I read, and today it still holds a place dear to my heart. If you have no prior knowledge of markets, Peter will show you '*How To Use What You Already Know To Make Money In The Market.*'

Tony Robbins' book, *Money: Master The Game* is possibly the largest compilation of interviews and advice from investing masterminds on paper. Tony sets out a seven-step plan for your financial freedom and talks you through each one in an easy to understand way. I certainly recommend you give it a read!

Joel Greenblatt's book, *The Little Book That Still Beats The Market* is probably the easiest read of all and a great book for beginners to get their hands on, it can be read in one sitting and is actually pretty funny!

Leverage Foreign Exchange

Does the idea of exchanging currencies fill you with fear and dread? I worked in the foreign exchange markets for seventeen years, so hopefully I can offer you some practical insights.

The worry of different currencies seems to strike fear into many people's hearts as they feel they don't want to be ripped off or lose out to bad exchange rates. The topic of Forex comes up almost weekly on different travel forums and FB pages, and there is always a plethora of differing information.

The stress levels this causes people is too high and I hope I can appease your troubled minds with a very basic understanding of how the markets work and how the banks and exchange companies conduct their business to make their money.

Firstly, it's important to know that the rates we see as consumers are very far away from what is referred to in the financial markets as the 'Spot Rate'.

The Spot Rate is the rate at which the world's largest banks and huge conglomerates are dealing with each other in multi-millions of dollars every second of every day. In terms of the volume (amount) traded day-to-day, the FX market is BY FAR the largest market in the world.

How can you play the game and get the best rate for

you and your family? Well, you can also see the spot rate on the internet, it's not a secret! Simply Google the currency pair you want to exchange and you will be hit with lots of different sites quoting the up-to-date spot rate. I generally check www.XE.com. Others you can find are:

- www.reuters.com
- www.bloomberg.com
- www.googlefinance.com
- www.yahoofinance.com

It's super important that you understand that competition for business in this market is super high and you, as the customer, have great power.

Once you are armed with the information of the real price, you can negotiate the rate with almost any entity in which you choose to engage to change your money. Yes, even at the currency exchange booths in an airport (the worst place to change currency). Always ask for a better rate than you are quoted in the first place.

The vendors make their money from what we call 'The Spread.' Each time you look at an exchange rate board you will see the columns 'We Buy' and 'We Sell'. The difference between these prices is called 'The Spread.'

The vendor will be quoting this spread right around the middle of the real market 'Spot Rate' that the banks are quoting to each other.

Now let's look at how the vendor is making their money. As they are dealing with Foreign Exchange all day, the vendor will accrue huge sums of different currencies that they will need to change to their home currency. The vendor will have a professional trading account set with the large banks' trading desks where they can get instant access to the spot rate to offset any transactions they make.

Therefore, the wider the spread, the more money they stand to make from any transaction. Always look at the spread to see how wide it is. The wider it is, the more room you have for negotiation.

Let's use a common currency pair as an example: Great British Pounds (GBP) vs. United States Dollars (USD). Let's say Jake is travelling from the UK to the USA for a holiday, so he needs to sell GBP to buy USD. He has saved one thousand pounds for his trip and is going to use that money to get the USD he needs to spend when he is there.

He checks the spot rate on www.xe.com by typing in the two currency pairs, GBP and USD, and sees that the rate is 1.2600. This simply means that for every £1 GBP that Jake sells, he will receive $1 USD and 26 cents… or $1.26.

Multiply that rate by the amount of GBP he is selling and he will get the total amount of USD he will receive:

1000 x 1.2600 = 1260.00 USD

But, Jake will not get to see that rate because the spot rate is only reserved for the huge banks and conglomerates that are trading in millions and billions each minute. They simply don't have time to do every FX transaction in the world.

This is where independent vendors and high street banks step in. Let's break down how the vendor will make their money with a quick example. After his two seconds of research, Jake is armed with knowledge and knows exactly what the spot rate is. He walks into a high street foreign exchange vendor to check the rates and sees:

GBP v USD

'We Buy' 1.2100 v's 'We Sell' 1.3100 (a spread of 10 cents)

(The rate GBP is bought in exchange for USD) versus (The rate GBP is sold in exchange for USD). Jake sells his 1000 GBP at the rate of 1.2100

1000 x 1.2100 = $1210.00 USD

Jake walks out of the exchange with $1,210 USD.

The next customer, Jane, needs to do the opposite to Jake and wants to sell her USD to buy 1000 total of GBP. To make this exchange, the vendor will use the 'We Sell' rate of 1.3100 for this transaction.

1000 x 1.3100 = $1310.00 USD

Jane has to part with all $1310 USD to get the £1000 GBP. The vendor's profit lies between the two transactions.

$1310.00 USD - $1210.00 USD = $100 USD profit

All of that for doing pretty much nothing! You can imagine how these volumes can move into the millions and billions very quickly as people are changing money every second of every day.

So how can you shop around for the best rate? I use www.compareholidaymoney.com to get a clear picture of exactly which vendors are offering what rates. The rates are listed in order of best to worst and, I guarantee you, your high street bank or credit card provider is waaaaaay down the list.

After finding this list, I started calling each company to ask them if I was able to set up an account or do a one-time transfer with them. In some cases, it's not possible, but others were only too happy to help and I was now exchanging money as close to the spot rate as you will ever get.

Don't forget, even when dealing with these companies that are showing you a much fairer rate, you still hold the power. Always ask for better. The worst they can say is "no". Most times they will improve the rate just a tiny bit to keep you happy and to keep your business.

I have also found two other companies that are totally web-based, easy to set up, provide better rates than almost anyone on the street and charge very low fees.

- www.transferwise.com
- www.currencyfair.com

If you want to try Currency Fair, I have set up an account with them and have been impressed with their prices and service, fees are set to just $3 U.S. per transaction.

Please feel free to use my referral code for a test run to see how you like their service!
(www.currencyfair.com/?channel=RVWJ31)

I have just been introduced to possibly the easiest service I have found so far, in the form of a prepaid travel card. We are currently witnessing a huge disruption in the banking sector due to the advent of Fintech companies entering the space offering huge savings, and far better usability to the public.

I recently learnt about www.revolut.com and have been very impressed with their offering. Simply transfer some money onto your Revolut account and use the virtual or physical card whenever you are travelling. They exchange your money at the exact spot rates usually reserved for the interbank market, without fees! They are always updating their service and, after a funding round in July of 2017 that raised $66 million, you can bet they have some great new services coming!

Simply make a quick payment from your debit card to your account and hop on the plane, no need to exchange physical money or risk carrying lots of foreign currency around with you.

You can set up an account by downloading the Revolut app on IOS or in the play store in a matter of minutes. Follow this link (https://revolut.com/r/daniel5q1) to open your account and start saving!

A Forgotten Source of Cash

Another one of those frequently asked questions we get is from the folks who ask -- almost awestruck -- How did you sell everything? And don't you miss your belongings?

Oh, how attracted and attached we are to stuff! And that really is all it is at the end of the day, stuff.

We are a consumer driven society fanned into a frenzy of buy, buy, buy, even if we don't need it, just buy it, it's on sale and if you can't afford it just buy it anyway on credit! Before you know it, you have a house full of stuff that owns you rather than you owning it.

Let's take a look at a typical family with two kids who receive gifts for birthdays and Christmas and think about how much stuff might walk through your doors over the course of just one year. I guarantee you that each kid ends up with at least ten presents each per birthday, whether they are books, puzzles, trikes, Barbies, Legos, whatever it might be. Then, once all gifts have been opened from grandparents, aunties, friends, etc., another twenty presents each at Christmas time.

That is a whopping sixty different pieces of junk

ending up in cupboards, never to see the light of day again. Then multiply that by twenty years!

Here is another experiment: go and count how many pieces of underwear you have in your house right now. Socks, pants, bras, vests, whatever it might be that you class as underwear. You will be astounded. You could clothe a small army!

Do the same for chairs. Walk around and count how many seating options you have in your house, don't forget the kitchen stools, garden furniture, spare chairs in the shed or attic, dining chairs, sofas and that chair in your bedroom under a pile of clothes, the seat in front of the vanity mirror, the piano stool, etc. Go ahead, add them all up. I bet you could host the next town hall meeting.

How many TVs do you have? Most households have more TVs than people!

As overwhelming as it may be to recognise just how much unnecessary junk you have filling up your life, the good news is that getting rid of it will also help you to make a little extra cash....

We started selling our stuff because we had to. We had a move to make and loads of un-needed items to sell, but I wish we had done it a hell of lot earlier. I wish we had done an annual cull because the clutter you acquire is incredible.

We spent hours deciding on our plan of action and walked around the house with a clipboard, making a note of everything we definitely wanted to keep. For example, we had some very specific pieces of furniture and artwork that were unique to our lives and wanted for ourselves again one day. Some pieces we stored with family, others we gave to friends to furniture sit for us on the understanding that we could get it back one day if we wanted it.

Once we had our list completed, we set to work selling the rest. There are several ways to sell your belongings over the internet, such as eBay, Gumtree, Craigslist and Facebook.

Then, of course, you have the traditional garage sales from your home, boot sales organised nearby, or other local markets or bazaars where you can pay for a stall and sell whatever you need to. We tried all of these methods and had great success. Anything we couldn't sell but needed to part with we donated to charity.

We sold huge pieces of furniture, book cases, wardrobes, cabinets, coffee and side tables, furniture, the BBQ and our sofa set. We sold the washing machine, tumble dryer, dishwasher, fridge, vacuum cleaner, TVs, DVD players, stereo systems, power tools, rugs, beds, cots, high chairs, strollers, car seats, bikes, scooters, golf clubs, clothes and the car.

Even the kids became hooked. The toys they wanted and begged for us to keep were all sold, by the kids themselves, at garage sales. The whole family was on board and in full clear-out mode.

The effect it had to our mindset was amazing, the less clutter we had around us, the clearer we could think. It actually became highly addictive. The fact that we were making money from things we didn't want any more also helped keep up our momentum, every penny made was going to hold us in good stead over the next year!

I highly recommend you keep a spreadsheet of everything you sell. We did, down to the last item, and we were stunned to come to the huge total of 15,000 Singapore dollars.

We couldn't believe it. All of that 'stuff' gone from our lives, and in return we had a clearer mind, we were a lot happier and we had extra money to travel with!

Do not underestimate the value of the 'stuff' you have in your house and don't even consider the pointless money pit of paying for storage. Why would you pay for your 'stuff' again in storage fees? If you ever return you can soon enough buy new stuff, or second-hand items. But I can guarantee that once it's gone, you will likely never want it back again anyway!

Go ahead, throw a garage sale and see how you feel afterwards. I bet you will feel lighter, more energised, happier and motivated!

Wants V. Needs

"I'd like to tidy up the entire planet. I would go anywhere if there were something that needs tidying."
- Marie Kondo

Finally, let's get a little deeper here with how much money you actually need to live a happy life. When you are going through the clear out phase of your home and possessions, a huge realisation hits you: You don't actually need any of this crap.

In her book, *The Life Changing Magic of Tidying Up*, Marie Kondo has gained a cult following of 'declutterers' and minimalists. Through her KonMari method she simply asks this one question of you. 'Does the object you hold in your hand spark joy inside of you?' If not, you don't need it, get rid of it. And that doesn't mean squirrel it away in that cupboard of death with all your other crap that hasn't seen the light of day in years, it means get rid of it.

Once we went through our own huge fire sale, I came to realise that there is a huge difference between a want and a need. I also came to realise that buying things for people just because it's Christmas and is deemed socially acceptable for a person to have a present to open on Christmas morning is utterly pointless. Why would somebody bother going to the effort and expense of buying me handkerchiefs, socks, music CDs or books that I will likely never ever look at again? It doesn't bring me any happiness at all, in fact, it brings nothing but disappointment and confusion.

A want is just that, a want. A need, however, is much more powerful. Once you break it down to its bare bones, all any of us actually need is clean water, without that we are dead in about three days. Forget food, you can last months without it. Water is your base for which you can start layering on top all of your other needs. Shelter, food, clothing and up the tree we go, all the way to a sixty-four-inch flat screen TV with satellite sports coverage and of course the chauffeur driven Bentley.

Go ahead, test yourself. Do you want a car, or do you need a car? Most people living in cities or urban areas don't need a car at all. Public transport is usually more than good enough, walking is likely a possibility in many cases. If not, there are many options such as taxis, ride sharing, bicycles and so on.

But we want that car, we want everything it stands for, and not only that we want the one we can't afford. We want the Mercedes, the BMW or the Porsche. It tells everybody we are rich and we are successful, then we want another car, for our spouse, or for times when we want to go on a shorter or longer journey. Whereas, in the countryside, where people actually need and totally depend on a car, they are driving from A to B in a twenty-year old trusty wagon.

Do you want that new iPhone 7s with the extra screen inches and memory space? Or do you need to be able to contact somebody in case of an emergency, and honestly, when have you ever experienced such an emergency when you needed to contact somebody?

Do you want that new pair of shoes, suit, dress, handbag, watch or necklace, or do you need it?

Ask yourself from now on, before you buy anything, 'Is this a want or a need', you will likely start spending a lot more wisely!

— — — — — — — — — — —

Thoughts From Clair

For me, getting rid of all our things was hard. We had a house full of stuff and hundreds of toys for children of three different age groups and developmental stages. Because Dan was still at work during this period, it was mostly down to me, in addition to all my other daily jobs, to get rid of everything. But on top of all this, I liked my stuff! I wouldn't go as far as to say that I'm a hoarder, but I don't like to waste and I find it hard to throw things away. Dan, on the other hand, found it really easy, freeing even.

We had a few large furniture pieces taken away to be auctioned in the beginning and then we did our first garage sale. I did feel that as soon as these items were gone that I didn't miss them one bit. We had more space, a little bit of spare cash and I was starting to get the hang of it and got great joy from receiving money for old items.

It was time consuming though. I put things up for sale on Craigslist and on Facebook groups. Most people that came to buy things were lovely, kept their appointment and paid the agreed price, but there were also a lot of time wasters and people that wanted to get something for nothing. It's quite difficult when you are trying to sell a good quality, well-loved item that means a lot to you only to have somebody lowball you to test your desperation to sell.

There were a few large furniture items that we had bought in Asia that we just wouldn't be able to replace and I wanted to keep. So, we arranged a part container shipment back to the UK and had planned on looking into storage, but family kindly offered to store them in lofts or garden sheds. I also wanted to keep a few sentimental items that meant a lot to the kids and some of my better-quality shoes, bags or clothes. Otherwise, the rest of our household items were sold, given to charity or given to friends.

Overall, it was a great experience to go through and one we all learnt a great deal from.

TOOLS AND TRICKS

There are a ton of money saving techniques that I could go into, but why do that when I can point you to the experts?

The best ever presentation I have seen on how the economy works is by Ray Dalio, one of the most well-respected fund managers of all time. https://www.youtube.com/watch?v=PHe0bXAIuk0

Learn the wonders of compounding interest with this very easy to understand video from Sal Khan
https://www.khanacademy.org/economics-finance-domain/core-finance/interest-tutorial/compound-interest-tutorial/v/introduction-to-compound-interest

Possibly the most fervently followed blog around money

saving is that of Mr. Money Moustache: https://www.mrmoneymustache.com/ a thirty-something retiree who cut out as much of the expensive living style he could to lead a 'frugal, yet badass life of leisure!'
Twitter @mrmoneymoustache

You can also look into people such as:
Martin Lewis from www.moneysavingexpert.com or @MartinSLewis
Suze Orman suzeorman.com @SuzeOrmanShow
Dave Ramsey www.daveramsey.com @DaveRamsey

www.udemy.com is a website aimed at adults where you can choose from over 40,000 potentially life-changing online courses across multiple subjects. You may be overwhelmed by the choices.

Do you want to learn more from the best? Just reach out and say hello. Seriously, what do you have to lose?
www.thefourhourworkweek.com - @tferriss
www.sethgodin.com
http://www.iwillteachyoutoberich.com - @ramit
www.Appsumo.com - @Noahkagan

www.michelle-holmes.com is where you can find Michelle and reach out about essential oils or mentoring

www.realvisiontv.com @ttmygh for Grant Williams @RaoulGMI for Raoul Pal https://www.tonyrobbins.com/ - @TonyRobbins

https://www.youtube.com/watch?v=9XRPbFIN4lk Ted talk by Adam Baker titled 'Sell your crap. Pay your debt. Do what you love.'

One Up On Wall Street by Peter Lynch
https://www.amazon.com/One-Up-Wall-Street-Already/dp/0743200403

Money: Master The Game by Tony Robbins -

https://www.amazon.com/MONEY-Master-Game-Financial-Freedom/dp/1476757860/ref=sr_1_1?s=books&ie=UTF8&qid=1502848035&sr=1-1&keywords=money+master+the+game

The Little Book That Still Beats The Market by Joel Greenblatt - https://www.amazon.com/Little-Book-Still-Beats-Market/dp/0470624159/ref=sr_1_1?s=books&ie=UTF8&qid=1502848117&sr=1-1&keywords=that+little+book+that+still+beats+the+market

The Life Changing Magic Of Tidying Up by Marie Kondo
https://www.amazon.com/Life-Changing-Magic-Tidying-Decluttering-Organizing/dp/1607747308

Further reading I suggest on entrepreneurship *The $100 Startup* by Chris Guillebeau
https://www.amazon.com/100-Startup-Reinvent-Living-Create/dp/0307951529

Chris spent months trawling through data of entrepreneurs who supplied him with information on how they started and ran their businesses. The book is extremely well written and a great tool guide for anybody looking to set up their own sideline business.

Further reading on 'selling your stuff', I recommend *Stuffocation, Living More With Less* by James Wallman - https://www.amazon.com/Stuffocation-James-Wallman/dp/1909979007

In his book, he discusses the rise of the minimalist culture and experientialist families who are forging a path to a more fulfilling life through experience rather than materialism. He also grounds you with the history of how we got where we are today, the problem of stuffocation and the throw away consumer driven culture that we have become.

Sites to check into FX rates:

Referral link to Revolut https://revolut.com/r/daniel5q1

An independent blog post about prepaid travel or currency cards which you can use to compare your best options. https://www.moneysavingexpert.com/credit-cards/prepaid-travel-cards

Referral link for Currency Fair
www.currencyfair.com/?channel=RVWJ31

- www.transferwise.com
- www.compareholidaymoney.com
- www.XE.com
- www.bloomberg.com
- www.googlefinance.com
- www.yahoofinance.com
- www.worldwidecurrencies.com

If you are interested in buying some crypto currency check out Coin Hako and follow my referral link to earn yourself a free $5!
https://www.coinhako.com/referrals/sign_up/DANIELPRIN_736331

Chapter 7
Travelling With Kids

"And let me tell you something. That first morning, when you are in your country of choice, away from all of the conventions of atypical, everyday lifestyle, looking around at your totally new surroundings, hearing strange languages, smelling strange, new smells, you'll know exactly what I'm talking about. You'll feel like the luckiest person in the world."
- Rolf Potts

Pop, fizz, whoosh.

The cork ejected itself from the bottle neck and flew straight into the air forming a perfect arc across the patio before gently landing on the freshly mown lawn. The gathered families cheered and whooped and the children screeched with delight. The bubbles started flowing and the long awaited catch up with old friends began in earnest.

It's been pretty funny over the last few years how we have been exposed to the same line of questioning at such gatherings. One of my favourite questions to answer is the one that goes like this:

"How on earth do you do spend all day every day with your kids? It would drive me freaking nuts! One weekend and I am done, it's more than enough!"

To be perfectly honest, if I look back without donning a pair of rose tinted glasses, I almost certainly used to feel like this too. Thinking deeper about it now, and with the fortune of hindsight and experience, I think I can probably answer this question much more admirably than the stock answer of, "Oh, you end up getting used to the little shits."

If I look back at my previous life and think how I used to feel at that time, it makes more sense. For parents in full-time employment, you get to the end of the week knackered and the parent who has been holding down the fort at home for the week will also be equally tired.

Your Friday nights would have been unceremoniously diminished to a wish that the children settle early enough, for you to catch at least one episode of a DVD box set, with a take away meal on your lap, before falling into bed praying for a full night's sleep.

It's terrible, isn't it?

Your Saturdays and Sundays are then generally mashed together by activities such as random kids' parties, sporting commitments, clubs, play dates, grocery shopping, DIY and other general crap that grinds you into the floor.

By 3 p.m. on a Sunday your internal fear gauge starts rising, and you start a slow descent into the anxiety of that Monday morning feeling. By dinner time, you are in full resentment mode, and any misbehaviour or refusal of bedtime gets met with a horrible response.

You subsequently start your week on a total downer, having spent what you perceive to have been a shit weekend, with a wife and kids who are systematically plotting against you to ruin your life.

Awful huh?

Once I had left my career and we started travelling as a family, the adjustment for all of us was huge. It was weird that I was now around the whole day and part of every on-the-spot parental decision. The family had to make adjustments for that just as much as I had to. I found my patience grew better over time, but there were some huge blow ups and stress to deal with for all of us.

Personally, I found the mundane arguing, bickering and general three eight-year-old childlike behaviour to be unbearable at times. However, in a moment of clarity, I realised that I had had to deal with this behaviour all day in an office environment too. We all do. We all have those colleagues that drive us nuts, unbearable bosses or intolerable customers behaving like spoilt kids. At least this was now on my terms and with people I actually loved and cared for!

What we have found over the last few years of being so closely knit together is that we have a much deeper understanding of our kids' personalities. We understand how differently they learn, what they respond to best and are naturally passionate about. We know when to push and when to change tack.

More than anything, we know that they are growing up with the solid support of their parents being there every day for them to wake up to, spend all day with and say goodnight to. That, in itself, is priceless.

But, I know you are still wondering just how challenging it is to travel with children. Many people choose not to travel when they have children because they prefer not to find out. We have lost count of how many times we have been asked the following questions:

But how do you travel with all the kids? Are they okay with it? Do they get travel sick? Do they behave on the plane? What do you take to keep them amused?

Followed by the same excuses for not travelling themselves: We can't travel because the kids just won't sit still. It would be too stressful. It's just too much hassle.

But these are just excuses. If you don't want to travel, then don't travel. That's cool. But don't hide behind your children and project your own fears and worries onto them. If you asked 100 kids if they wanted to get on an airplane and spend a week in a different country or state, I bet 90% would jump at the chance.

Travelling with children is a huge subject and one that's debated and talked about constantly within the travel community. Travel magazine AFAR once graciously invited me to write an article about this exact subject. I have included the article below with some extra tidbits of wisdom we've picked up since it was published. Hopefully it will allay some of your fears and kick start you into getting out there and spending some quality family time together.

If truth be told, you might never run out of excuses and you probably won't find the answer to all of the questions. But the point is, the answers will only present themselves and come to you as you travel.

No matter what, remember this: Travelling and flying

with kids is no biggie—just get going, enjoy the ride and experience the adventure together!

1. **DO NOT** overthink or overhype it. Don't even tell your kids you're going away until a few weeks or even days before. There is nothing worse than having young children revelling in the idea of getting on a plane for months on end.

Why?

Because, come the actual moment of boarding and sitting down, the expectation built up in their minds will be chronically smashed causing anxiety and frustration. This will lead to fidgety behaviour and endless questioning.

In your impressionable young child's mind's eye, they would never have imagined that getting on a plane would ever be as boring as getting strapped into an uncomfortable seat so that they can't move. All they can see is the back of the seat in front and, even if they were sat next to the window, it is too high for them to see out of without kneeling up, which of course gets met with 'just sit down nicely.' The kid is bored to tears and pissed off that flying on a plane, which they thought was going to be so wonderful, is actually crap.

So, do not overhype it!

2. **DO** (whenever possible) choose a flight time when the kids are not likely to be tired. Boarding a plane at 10 p.m. will always end in tears.

3. **DO NOT** let them 'run around to burn off some energy before boarding the flight. A quick fact for you: if you exercise, your body releases endorphins and adrenaline, which makes you feel great and keeps you wired for hours after the activity. If you encourage your child to run around before a flight, you can't then expect the child to go and sit down and not move for a number of hours. Just ask any school teacher how painful the first lesson after lunch break is!

Allowing your kids to play tag and run recklessly around the airport is just a no-no. Keep them calm, take strolls up and down the waiting area, watch the airplanes and airport vehicles buzz around outside, watch the TV in the boarding area. Do anything other than harsh physical stimulation.

4. **DO NOT** bring 1000+ toys/books/teddies/games in your carry-on. Let them discover their new surroundings before you give them toys. Let them be free with their

inquisitive process and follow their lead.

We found our three-year-old twins loved to sit down and belt themselves up before leafing through the pocket of magazines in front of them. Their absolute favourite thing was the laminated safety instructions. Why? Because it's covered with pictures of people shooting down a massive slide! We used to get a full story out of them as they went through each picture telling us what was going on. They even named the characters after family members.

Then, they'd move onto the inflight duty-free shopping magazine. Why? Because it's filled with bright colourful pictures of toys, perfumes, watches, sweets, and its glossy pages were wonderful to touch. Plus, they felt grown up and a part of the crowd—this is what everybody else was doing around them.

5. **DO** buy sticker books. There is a sticker album for every age and every topic, sport, hobby, TV show/pop star out there. You will know which ones they'll love and you can buy them right there in the airport without them even knowing. They are light, inexpensive, and wonderful fun to a child.

I suggest waiting until after takeoff and slipping the albums in the seat pocket when they're not looking. Try guiding them to discover it for themselves, which will give them the sense that they have found it and experience the wonderful surprise of it being their favourite character. This works on a much better level than just being handed something and told to 'Be a good boy, just play with your sticker book.'

6. **DO** bring snacks. NO SWEETS, CHIPS OR COOKIES! Are you insane? Who in their right mind can expect a child that has just been stuffed full of sugar to sit still? I cringe when I see other parents doing this. To be honest, the airlines themselves really need to snap out of it and start taking the chocolate and cakes out of the kids' meals. It's just a recipe for disaster.

We always travel with some of the following snack items: Crunchy cucumber and carrot sticks, cubed cheddar cheese, apples, and dried fruit or nuts. All can be prepared at home and put in a Ziploc bag or small Tupperware. Believe me, if they are hungry, they will eat it, especially if you start eating it first.

7. **DO** enlist the help of electronics. A great tip is to secretly download a new album or app for them to discover. This will kill hours of time and put a huge smile on their faces.

If the flight is long haul, the inflight entertainment systems are unbelievable. There are hundreds of movies, TV shows, games and music to choose from. Let them enjoy being able to watch TV or play games for hours on end!

8. **DO** try and get them to sleep. When you see that first yawn, you have to pounce. Whip out that favourite bedtime teddy, offer a quick cuddle, stroke their hair, and watch them drift off into sleepy land.

9. **DO** treat yourself to that glass of wine or beer from the drinks trolley. Sit back and relax—you're going on holiday!

Since I wrote this article, we have learned a few other actionable points from which you can definitely benefit. They are more travel hacks than kid advice, but definitely worth applying!

Look at your luggage options. Especially if you need to book hold luggage with a budget airline, make sure you check the site rules. On many occasions, we have managed to book a suitcase on a child's ticket for half price, then crammed hand luggage as full as possible and offered to check it for free at the check in desk. The check in staff will thank you for being so generous in helping them to keep bags out of the overhead bins, when really, you'll have just got 50 kilos of luggage shipped for the price of one suitcase!

Never pay extra for allocated seating, the prices seem cheap but soon rack up if you are buying multiple seats for the family. The airlines will try and trick you into fearing you will be seated apart, and they will win many of those fear battles I am sure, but stay strong! We have been seated apart on several flights and have always found the person sat next to our child has not hesitated in agreeing to swap seats with us. People really are very nice if you smile and ask politely!

Take full advantage of travelling with kids! Early boarding times are always extended to families, so get up to the front of the queue and politely check with the cabin crew half an hour before boarding time. They will likely show you to a reserved seating area and board you with the business class passengers during the first call just to get the kids out of the line and into a buckled seat!

Always pack your own food, even on long haul international flights. There is nothing like a homemade sandwich or salad to help you through the journey. Airline food is terrible at best and if you are buying food on the budget airlines, you are way overspending on total rubbish.

Pack an empty bottle for water and ask the friendly cabin crew if they wouldn't mind filling it up for you, paying the highly inflated prices on board is not an option!

We learnt a rather unique travelling trick New Year's Day 2015. We were on a pretty empty commuter bus travelling back to our home swap from our friend's house in Sydney. We were getting ready with the cameras as we approached to cross the famous harbour bridge, when suddenly our daughter Sophia announced she didn't feel too well.

Poor Sophia suffers from travel sickness and even though this had been a simple bus ride, a mix of the excitement and late night before had piled up on her. As Clair and I scrambled to find some sick bags, the man in front of us whipped around and asked in an accusatory manner

"Does she get travel sick, is she going to be sick?"

What do you say to such a direct question, and at the same time appease them that they won't get chundered on?

"Er, well, yeah, sometimes she gets a little queasy, but hopefully she will be okay now, it's not far to go."

The guy looked straight at Sophia and held his hands up at her. "Do this, start scrunching your fingers, you see how I am doing it? Now do the same with your toes, really start scrunching your toes together, and take some deep breaths, how does that feel?"

Sophia answered that she felt a little better. "Okay good, keep doing it for the rest of the journey, scrunching your fingers and your toes and taking deep breaths, you will soon forget you feel sick!"

He then turned to myself and Clair and explained that when he was growing up, his brother had suffered terribly from motion sickness. His parents had tried everything to help him, but all of the lotions and potions were just pointless. It wasn't until they found a specific doctor that they learnt this technique, and were amazed at how it worked.

We still use this technique whenever the kids feel a little motion sickness. Even I have used it to settle my stomach on bumpy airplane journeys or boats. It doesn't work every time, but it is certainly effective and has, without doubt, saved us many pukes!

It is quite likely that you will still run into issues during a flight, bus ride, train ride, or anywhere you might go. After answering so many 'worry questions' over the years, it has become obvious to us that there is a huge amount of fear and stigma attached to travelling with kids. From what I have learnt it seems people experience the terrible self-deprecating demons that have a horrible habit of entering your mind.

Why are you are disturbing the people around you?

Everybody is looking at you and judging the behaviour of your family! You clearly don't have control over your children!

Why won't that child stop crying?

Why can't you do something about it?

Why is your child kicking the seat of the passenger in front?

Why won't that child sit nicely and be quiet?

Why are they running around and tripping people up in the queue?

Why do they need to go to the toilet now?

The list goes on, doesn't it?

"I have several times made a poor choice by avoiding a necessary confrontation."
- John Cleese

A strange phenomenon we have encountered when travelling with children is the fact that almost all other nationalities love kids and want to be around them, ask them questions, talk with them, and watch them play and, in many cases, have pictures taken with them.

For some reason, and I am going to pick on fellow Britishers here, we seem to have this ingrained notion that kids should be seen but not heard. And it's real. Each time we travel through England, we feel the awful glares and overhear the audible sighs and comments as we sit down at a table in a restaurant, take our seats in a cinema, arrive at a pub or board a train or bus. It makes us feel horrible and raises our stress levels. We feel we have to be on top of our 'parenting' and make sure the kids are behaving as if under the stewardship of Mary fucking Poppins!

Shit then rolls downhill, we start over-parenting and acting unnaturally, which confuses the kids and prompts them to react strangely back to us, causing a closed loop of increased stress and anxiety due to the perceived 'public shaming.'

Why does it have to be this way?

In many other countries around the world it is generally the complete opposite. In Asia, for example, the stress and anxiety is caused by people overjoyed at seeing young white skinned and fair-haired children. Throw in blue eyes and you have real trouble! They want pictures of themselves with your children, want to hug them, kiss them and connect with them. They ask questions in perfectly broken English and want them to sit on their laps or offer them sweets. At first, it's a little off putting, but if you step back and think about it, it's actually quite wonderful.

We discovered the perfect middle ground is to be found in countries such as Spain, Italy and Croatia. When travelling through theses destinations the local people tend to be endearing toward the children, but at the same time not overpowering.

Italian ladies have asked us if our son would like to sit on their laps whilst on crowded buses. Croatian people would befriend our family instantly, speaking with the kids, asking if they would like some food, ice creams or offering to take us to lunch or discounted sightseeing trips.

When in Spain we found the locals loved just watching kids be kids, whether it was ours, their own or somebody else's. They love sitting back over a drink and some tapas and watching the kids run rings around each other, through the tables, along the streets or around the squares. To them it's normal, they love seeing the kids playing and being happy and understand they will make noise and be boisterous. They embrace and encourage it.

Maybe a fear of travelling with children stems from

this Anglicised and Americanised feeling of having the perfect poster child that is going to respect their elders by calling them sir or madam, sitting perfectly still in a cramped airplane, bus or train seat and never suffering from acute boredom.

Or maybe we all need to get over ourselves and just let kids be kids. Wouldn't then the world be a happier place? Do not fear travelling with your children.

Park your fears and get going. It's too important not to!

TOOLS AND TRICKS

Original article in Afar Magazine:
http://www.afar.com/magazine/a-pros-tips-for-flying-with-kids-in-9-easy-steps

Link to the book, *Vagabonding*, by Rolf Potts whose quote opened this chapter: https://www.amazon.com/Vagabonding-Uncommon-Guide-Long-Term-Travel/dp/0812992180

Chapter 8
Shitty Travel Advice

"Wise men don't need advice. Fools won't take it."
- Benjamin Franklin

We were in a home swap situated right on the Norfolk Broads in England, We were loving this beautiful part of the world and the amazing winter weather. On this particular morning, the mist was still hanging over the water, which was banked by our garden where the ground frost was a brilliant white. The sun had started to shine and, slowly, the unshaded parts of the lawn were turning into patches of green. Cast in front of us was a picture-perfect winter scene.

I finished my breakfast and started checking the day's admin, emails, Twitter and Facebook accounts. Thanks to the latest attack of targeted advertising, I was subjected with the usual barrage of travel headlines and spam.

"Ten best things to do in Dubai."
"How to pack lightly."
"London in a day."

The headlines out there are truly endless. If you Google 'Travel Advice' you are inundated with different options. What's worse, the top hits generally include government warnings about where NOT to travel, driving fear into your very core.

Then there are the pretty dreadful blogs that are doing their very best trying to win the race to the bottom of the SEO (Search Engine Optimisation) game, hiring freelancers from sites such as Upwork for as little as $5 per article to keep a constant flow of content coming through their blogs. The ruse is simple: write pieces that are largely useless to most people and generally packed full of keywords to win a higher ranking on Google searches.

Lest we forget, the mainstream media of newspapers and magazines are also releasing articles that have generally been written in ten minutes by some hack 'travel writer' stuck behind a desk banging an article out for an angry editor.

It seems that everywhere you look these days there are loads of half-assed articles written about travel tips, what to do and what not to do, how to pack, where to go and why, etc.

I sat there on the Norfolk Broads reading more of this spam over a cup of black English tea. At this point we were already almost two years into a constant travel lifestyle and I felt that I needed to address this issue of shitty travel advice.

Some of these tips are, of course, fine. But wouldn't you want to know how the 'experts' are doing it? I felt that others needed to hear from the people that have been travelling long term for years, people who live the tips, tricks and hacks day in and day out, rather than just once a year!

I deleted the spam and, with a fire in my belly, decided to launch a mission to get the lowdown and insider advice on this topic for once and for all. My plan was simple, reach out to as many of the world's most respected Travel Bloggers, Worldschoolers, Edventurers, and Digital Nomads (call them what you will) as I could and get their input. I got straight onto the Twittersphere and started compiling a list of the most influential travel individuals and engaged them.

To give you some idea of the collective reach of the awesome people who answered me with their advice, the travel gurus between them had a sum of 1,028,650 combined Twitter followers. That's quite a reach, especially considering these were just ordinary people who decided to leave the rat race and make a life for themselves. They weren't sponsored by a company or backed by magazines, they were making their own waves and engaging a global audience with their different views of life, family and travel.

Whilst they all came from many different backgrounds, had totally different family situations, had been born in completely different cultures and travelled to many different countries, they all have one thing in common: they have all been travelling for many years and offer bona fide, iron clad, proven, authoritative and expert advice from the front lines of extended travel and life on the road.

I got some great responses and all of them were only too happy to help. They agreed that it was a subject littered with wishy washy articles, not getting the real and proven information out there.

The tips and quotes I received aren't exactly what you would expect. Lots of answers go way deeper than the usual 'Set up alerts on Skyscanner' or 'Use go compare' to get the best rates blah blah blah rubbish. Some of the quotes are heartwarming, others inspiring, profound, powerful and hopefully, for some, life changing.

Feel free to get in touch with any of these individuals and families. They are super friendly and only too happy to help point you in the right direction! In the post on our blog PrincesOffTheGrid I have included the website and Twitter link to each awesome contributor, check it out and reach out to them. I bet they'll respond!

Enjoy the advice, thoughts and insights from the world's most travelled, but more importantly use it to your advantage, take action and get out there!

Enter, the experts... My question to each of them was thus:

"What is the best travel advice that you could give to somebody planning a trip that you actually use on your own travels?"

"I would say don't stress. Book your flight, buy your gear, and worry about the details right before you leave."
Matthew Kepnes @Nomadicmatt

"Get lost! Be prepared for your trip, but as soon you are in the destination, forget your itinerary, stay spontaneous and change your plans on the go. That's when the best things happen."
Melvin Bocher @Traveldudes

I love these two pieces of advice because we found it to be so true as we travelled. They also lend themselves perfectly to a metaphor for life. Staying flexible and open to change, seeking the paths less trodden and embracing spontaneity has opened so many doors and given us so many wonderful experiences. Just saying yes more often than no, not finding excuses to not do something and simply going with the flow has taken us completely out of our comfort zone many times, but each time has rewarded us with so much!

Our best example of this is accepting accommodation on a dairy farm in New Zealand in exchange for work. Not in our wildest dreams did we think we would ever find ourselves face to ass with 300 cows on a freezing cold morning at 6am whilst we milked them, but we did, and it was an amazing experience where we met some of the loveliest hosts and other travellers putting themselves out there.

"Fly on Wednesdays or Saturdays. These tend to be the cheapest days of the week to fly! Fridays and Sundays tend to be the most expensive days. As always, check within a range to see what's the cheapest."
Kate McCulley from AdventurousKate @Adventurouskate

Since getting Kate's advice, Google Flights really has upped the game for flight search engines and makes searching a lot less hassle. Kate is 100% right too, there are always cheaper days to fly and Google Flights even points out the cheaper days for that particular route or airline. Always check a few days in advance or after to see what you might be able to get!

"Best advice is to focus on cost saving in all aspects. I cover this more in my upcoming book. Low cost airlines booking ahead of time. Follow the right accounts on Twitter."
Henrik Jeppesen @Henriktravel

Henrik went on a mission to visit every country in the world, he did it, and he is still going! His website Henriktravel.com is a huge resource of information on how to travel low budget!

"Be nice to everyone."
Johnny Jet @JohnnyJet

So simple, but yet so effective. Just 'go first' with everybody you meet, be the first to smile, the first to bow, the first to offer your hand, the first to say good morning, hello, or good afternoon in the language of the native tongue. Be the first to say thank you, or please, be the first to offer your help to a lady crossing the road, be first to ask a stranger a question. Just always go first, you will find that amazing things happen when you do!

"Just book a ticket. When we first started looking to travel, or even now when we are looking of where to go next, research is always halfhearted. When you book the ticket, there is no return and working to a deadline is always much more inspiring."
Erin Bender @explorewitherin

Great advice from Erin! We once booked a ticket to France in the knowledge we only had accommodation for a certain amount of time, after that we had no idea where we might end up staying. But once we were on the ground, things slowly figured themselves out and we ended up housesitting for July and August in a beautiful part of the French countryside!

"Follow your heart. In other words, go where you're excited about, and do what inspires you, whenever you feel the call. Don't do something just because it makes sense, seems efficient, or is cost-effective. The former leads to fulfillment, even if things don't turn out the way you expect, and the latter leads to disappointment and regret, even if they do."
Brandon Pearce @Brandags

Brandon is completely right here, if you have a real pull to a destination then, damn it, just go! This is particularly powerful advice to myself as I sit here writing! We had been procrastinating over where to go for a two-month trip during July and August. Every bone in my body told me it made sense to stay in Europe, we could find home swaps or house sits, stay with family in England and drive to multiple locations.

However, there was a feeling in Clair and I that we wanted to be in Asia again. When we asked the kids what they wanted to do, they all chose to get back east too. We let our hearts rule the decision and we booked tickets to Bangkok. We are now busy lining up home swaps in and around Thailand. We are all currently thoroughly enjoying the feeling of anticipation and day dreaming of tasting the food again, re-exposing ourselves to the wonderful sights, smells, sounds and hustle of a totally different way of living and culture.

"Be prepared and organised when travelling, but don't overthink it. There are always things that can go wrong, but if you are well prepared then this should limit any problems. Worrying excessively will just stop you from having the trip of your life."
Sharon Gourlay @WheresSharon

    Sharon hits the nail on the head here, stop worrying, and don't let the fears take over. There are a million and one reasons you shouldn't do something, shut them all off, make a plan and go for it. The best experiences of your life wait just beyond that line of self-doubt!

I follow my advice in getting away from the tourist spots. I believe in "real" experience and hitting the road less travelled.
Michael Earle @Think Phuket

    This is great advice and a common mindset among the whole community. So many of us have experienced wonderful interactions with the locals in the places that we have visited. In fact, many of us would rather never return to a tourist spot or hotel again. This has been a huge part of our travel life through home swapping and one we are truly thankful to have had.

"You know, they say 'Strangers are just friends you don't know yet'. Don't be shy, just approach people first, use all the opportunities to meet the locals and you will be able to have the real experience of the country and hopefully understand the locals' mentality a bit better! You want to see the differences, to discover the real local culture, isn't that why we travel?"
Yulia @MissTouristCom

    Yulia's point can be coupled with @Johnnyjet's and my point of 'going first.'

"Never let others' opinion of a place decide your travels. Always experience a place for yourself & make your own opinion."
Charlie and Brittany @TradinTraveler

 I bet Charlie and Brittany have hit a nerve with you here. How many times have you been told to not watch a movie, not go to a certain restaurant, not to buy a certain thing, not to visit a certain place? Opinions are rife in our society today. If it's not your friends and family telling you what not to do, it will be mainstream media. Turn off the noise. Go anyway if you want to; you might just find that you will have the most amazing time.

 We were once advised to not to travel with the children on the subway in New York. The lady in question told us it was unsafe and that it was too dangerous. Under no circumstances should we do it, we would end up getting mugged, pick pocketed, abused or having one of the children snatched. Thankfully we did not listen to her advice and used the subway extensively all over the city and then out to the airport at the end of our trip.

 What happened? We met some really wonderful people who gave up their seats for the kids and helped us with directions and inside local knowledge.

"Don't over plan. Leave room for the unexpected."
Randi and Michael @JustaPack

 The unexpected will happen, but embrace it and it will become the norm and it is so enjoyable! I was once asked what I liked about travelling the most. I paused for the thought and reflected on the trip up to that point. It struck me that what I really loved was waking up each day and not knowing who we were going to meet that day, or what we might end up seeing.

 The fact that we were all in this together made it even more special. To think that the kids were waking up to a totally new day of adventure and experiential learning was an incredibly exciting prospect for me. There was no set routine, no set commute, no set rules, and no set expectations. We had learnt to expect the unexpected and we loved it (accidents and health issues aside of course!)

"Consider housesitting during your stay. Live rent free when you travel and immerse yourself in the local culture!"
Charli Moore from wanderlusters @wanderlustersUK

Amen! I have covered my thoughts on the sharing economy and the house sitting or swapping movement already me thinks?!

"Make sure you have enough ways to get access to money. Enough cards, and know what you'd do if you lost them all while away."
Dante Harker @DanteHarker

Practical advice from Dante. Supplementary credit cards are a great idea here. You can each travel with a card in separate safe places. If one does get lost, you still have the other to use. Note also to NEVER pay a credit card company a yearly subscription, not for the main card account or the supplementary card. In twenty years, I have never paid a fee. Once I notice the fees on the monthly statement I either make a quick phone call to the number listed on the back of the card or log in to my account and email the company directly requesting they waive the annual fees. Trust me, it works.

"When trying to book flights with my miles and points, I always search one-way at a time instead of round trip. Airline search engines don't always show everything that's available when searching round trips. Once I find and write down the flights I want, I call the airline to book. Be sure to tell them your itinerary wasn't bookable online to have phone reservation fees waived."
Jackie @Globetroteacher

We have used this advice to good effect too. Often times, if you call the airline directly they will match the cheap online price for you. It is effective at cutting out the middleman and gives you the opportunity to earn or cash in any airmile points you might have with that carrier.

It is so much easier to do if you are talking directly with a staff member taking the booking over the phone. We always tell them that we were unable to book online as we could not get through to payment as part of our family were flying with miles and the other part as payment. It's a loophole and one worth trying if you want to book directly with the airline.

"I always suggest that people consider ways they can earn money and travel at the same time. This has been our strategy for eighteen years and it's meant that our life has been one consistent travel journey. You don't have to save as much, you can travel longer, plus you have deeper and more enriching travel experiences."
Caz and Craig Makepeace @YTravelBlog

This is the goal for pretty much every travelling family we have met on the road. I have met so many different people making things work for themselves. Maybe it's a blog, an online business, freelancing Skype calls, or finding work along the journey.

"Don't over pack! Our bags keep getting smaller and lighter. Makes it so easy to travel on trains, load bags into taxis and lug up the stairs. I'm a firm believer!!"
Amber and Eric Hoffman @HusbandinTow

Hooooweee. This is the most common advice that is ever given by travellers to those who are just setting out. You could sum up the best advice like this:

Pack your bags, then unpack them, then pack them again, then unpack them, then pack them again. See how much that sucks? Now get rid of all the crap, there is nothing you can't buy when you get to a destination. Frankly you need the clothes on your back, a passport and a wallet.

As a family of six, we obviously had more than most and definitely over packed some articles, but that is bound to happen and it will happen again. Just try to be as ruthless as you can and know that everything will be alright when you get there!

I would actually love to do a travel challenge one day where I and a friend would turn up to an airport wearing nothing but a pair of boxer shorts with our passports in our hand. How far could we get? The naysayers immediately say we would be arrested. I don't believe that. I believe that out of the thousands of people there in the airport, you could beg a tee shirt, a pair of jeans and some flip flops in a matter of minutes. If not, you can get straight to the lost property room and see what has been unclaimed for years!

You would also find some kind people to loan you some of the local currency so that you could buy the cheapest one-way ticket available out of the country. Then you are fully on your way into the journey of faith in humanity. Now that's an adventure!

"Never book an overnight bus. This is one of those "fantastic ideas at the time", however in reality it's a terrible, no good, very bad idea!! The theory is that you'll make it from one place to another while saving on a night's accommodation. However, it's uncomfortable, you may think you're going to sleep but in all likelihood you're not, and barely getting any sleep, the first thing you do when arriving at your new accommodation is beg for an early check-in to get into the room! And your bright idea of making the most out of the next day is ruined with an afternoon nap which ends up wasting the day away. Take it from experience...the extra money it will cost for a flight is well worth the investment!"
Megan Jerrard @Mappingmegan

Getting this advice was actually great timing for us. As mentioned above, we are currently in the midst of planning through the logistics of our far eastern tour over the summer months and the option of an overnight sleeper train from Bangkok sounded like a great idea. Until, of course, I actually thought it through. It's a freaking dreadful idea! The journey of eighteen hours would be cramped, boring stressful and exhausting, it would have wiped us all out for days afterwards. The upside of saving a few hundred dollars just wasn't worth considering.

"When travelling on budget airlines with kids book your suitcases under a child's name, it is sometimes half price! Then pack as much as you can into carry on sized back packs and volunteer to check your carry-on luggage at the desk. They won't even check the weight as they are only too happy to keep bags out of the overhead cabins. You can now travel light

through the airport and have all your items transported at a fraction of the cost!"

Daniel and Clair Prince @Princey1976

—————————

TOOLS AND TRICKS

Here's the link to the blog post I wrote, which includes websites of all the above-mentioned contributors. Make sure to reach out and say hi if you are looking for further validation! http://princesoffthegrid.weebly.com/travel-blog/19-awesome-travel-tips-from-the-worlds-leading-travel-gurus

Chapter 9
It's Not All Fun in The Sun You Know!

> Too many of us are not living our dreams because we are living our fears.
> - Les Brown

We were tired and hot! The early afternoon breeze was a welcome cooling sensation as we sat by the pool overlooking the river watching fisherman lazily float past. We were in Chiang Mai in Northern Thailand and had just returned to our homestay after spending the day being shown around temples and driven to a Hill Tribe village high on the mountain where we had visited the primary school and watched some lessons in progress.

The twins were happily playing in the shallow overflow of an infinity pool and our elder daughters were reading books or doing crossword puzzles.

Then it happened.

First, I heard my wife scream, "Samuel, nooooooo!"

Then I heard Samuel screaming, a scream that every parent instantly knows is not the usual cry, it was a blood curdling scream of pure fear and pain.

We all jumped to our feet and ran towards him to assess the damage. During his play, he had attempted a jump that was far beyond his capabilities and had hit his head square on the side of the swimming pool wall.

His forehead had split open in an instant and we were looking straight into a horrible gash that had parted the tissue and was bleeding down between his eyes and over the tip of his nose.

Parental instincts kicked in, we applied basic first aid holding the gash together and trying to stem the blood flow whilst also trying to calm him.

I ran into the lobby, through the reception and straight into the home quarters of our hosts yelling for Yul, the Thai owner. He appeared immediately and listened as I explained the situation and asked if he could call an ambulance.

Thankfully Yul spoke perfect English (and French) and had been trained as a medic in the French army when he had lived in France as a young man. He told me to grab our passports and get into his car immediately.

It was not too far to the nearest hospital, but the drive was far from relaxing. Yul expertly showed his skill at dodging the numerous potholes, stray dogs, chickens and mopeds that darted in and out of the traffic and into his path.

After what seemed like a lifetime, but was likely only twenty minutes, we pulled into the hospital car park. Yul pulled the car around to the front of the building and stopped right outside the emergency department entrance. I threw the car door open and we rushed into the lobby with Samuel in my arms, still sobbing.

Yul quickly explained in Thai to the staff and doctors exactly what had happened, who we were, who he was, his own medical observations and what aid we had already administered.

Naturally, I understood nothing. Samuel's well-being was now purely at the mercy of fellow human beings from a different country and culture.

I held my son in my arms and looked into his eyes desperately trying to get him calmed. I tried my best to literally keep his head together, too; the wound had slowly been opening up more on the drive and was creeping down towards the bridge of his nose. The gash needed stitching and quick!

The nursing staff applied some bandaging and showed us into the waiting room where we seemed to sit for ages. Finally, we went through to see the doctor and Yul came with me as a translator.

The doctor advised me (via Yul) that, as it was a head injury, Samuel would have to stay overnight for observation.

This didn't seem right to me and I discussed this point in English with our host. We both agreed that the wound was superficial and Samuel had shown no bouts of dizziness, incoherence, headaches or sickness.

Yul and I both felt that this was just protocol from the hospital and I decided to sign the disclaimer form agreeing that I was responsible for Samuel's health once he left the hospital and that I acknowledged that I had turned down the overnight monitoring.

With the administrative aspects finished, we moved to the operating room and prepped for the stitches. The doctor advised us that if he could not get the anaesthetic into the wound via an injection, he would have to use gas. If that were the case, then we were staying for the night whether we liked it or not.

In an instant, Samuel was wrapped in a green surgical blanket to keep him from wiggling, flailing his arms around or kicking his legs. Two Thai medical staff and I held his body and head in total stillness as the doctor jabbed the anaesthetic straight into the open and gaping wound.

It was awful. His screams must have been heard throughout the whole building and it took every bone in my body to keep a brave and unwavering face for him to concentrate on.

Thankfully, the injections worked and the anaesthesia kicked in to numb the wound. The doctor and nurses got straight to work and expertly stitched up the wound whilst I talked constantly to Samuel, asking him questions, telling him stories, anything to keep his mind away from what was happening just above his eyes.

The doctor did an amazing job, he applied three stitches inside the wound to reattach tissue together and then eleven stitches on the surface of the wound to knit it all together, it probably only took fifteen minutes.

With the ordeal finally over, we were shown into the processing room where we waited for our bill. As we waited I called our travel insurance claims department and asked them what protocol I should follow. They advised me to pay for the treatment, keep the bills and then send the originals and a scanned copy via email to their address on the website once we had the opportunity.

Finally, we were called to the front window where we were given some bandaging and cream and the bill that amounted to $40 U.S!

$40 U.S.?!?

I couldn't believe it! It seemed too cheap for the level of care and attention they had given my son. But that was the entire bill! I paid, we left and I never bothered claiming the insurance!

Second Guessing

During that night and for a few weeks after the accident I was lost in a roller coaster of emotions. This was my fault. I had put him in danger, I had put them all in danger. It was my idea to take us all travelling, it was my idea to experience a different kind of life. I had been so wrapped up in my own desires that I had inadvertently put us all in a horrible situation.

My wife's confidence had also been knocked. She had experienced possibly the hardest situation after the initial accident as she watched me and Samuel disappear into the unknown world of a strange country and foreign hospital protocols whilst staying with our three young daughters. It was a very traumatic wait for our return and all of them were extremely worried and had no idea when we might return or how things had gone.

Many times, the thought crossed our minds that we should stop now before anybody else got hurt and we should get back to normal, comfortable everyday life again. It took some time for us to get our heads together to look at it rationally and, once again, put our fears aside.

Thankfully after a while we were able to look at it from a clearer perspective and gather our thoughts. The truth of the matter is that the accident could have happened anywhere, at any point or time in our lives, and probably something similar will happen again. It doesn't matter where you are in the world, it will take you by surprise and the only thing you can do is act appropriately when it does.

How many kids fall over in the school playground and need stitches to the head? This actually happened to me and my brother when we were kids in our home town's school yard, it happens every day in playgrounds across the globe. It's not a fear that should ever be considered when thinking about travelling.

Looking back at the situation now, and if I were to compare the same situation happening in an English-speaking country, the only true fear factor and uncomfortable part of the whole ordeal was not being able to communicate properly with the staff. The end result would have been the same in an English-speaking hospital, all that was different was the language barrier.

Why did I fear not being able to communicate?

We were in a hospital with highly trained individuals that stitch up injuries every day. The only thing standing between us was a language barrier — spoken words. Luckily for us, I had Yul there to help me. Even so, the highly trained doctor would have looked after and given our son the absolute best care if Yul had been there or not.

Don't doubt that at some point in your life some kind of emergency situation is going to instantly occur. Emergencies do not take into account the time of day, the age of the person or the place in the world where it will occur. You cannot wrap yourself in a cotton wool existence thinking that everything is just fine the way it is and feel that you are protecting yourself and your loved ones.

We have started to train ourselves to 'expect the unexpected'. I now walk around all day expecting a giant six-foot turd to fall from the sky straight onto my head, anything pulling up short of that is a walk in the park. Surely nothing can surprise me now, right?

And then another unexpected event happened. I was doubled up in pain whilst we were in New Zealand one night with what I thought was a dreadful bout of indigestion -- something I never suffer from. In the end, it actually turned out to be a burst appendix and resulted in an emergency appendectomy at the nearest (one-and-a-half-hours' drive away) hospital!

Rather than second guessing our choice to travel after this particular adventure, I realised that my appendix would have burst if I was still sat at my desk in my old job. It was just one of those things that was always going to happen. I couldn't control it, nobody could have even predicted it was going to happen, we just had to deal with it once we were presented with the emergency.

Medical Tourism

The subject of medical tourism has been discussed at length by many other writers and bloggers in the past, it is not a new concept and has been around for decades.

Among our family travel groups, I can't say that anybody in particular has been a medical tourist as such, but many of us have ended up accidentally becoming them!

As already highlighted, we found ourselves in a hospital situation with Samuel and an emergency operation for my appendectomy. We have also had to have our son's arm x-rayed as well as my oldest daughter's ankle, both because of random falls in playgrounds.

Other examples from the travel groups we belong to of medical help along the road ranges from generic doctor visits, broken bones, inoculations and dental visits all the way up to getting pregnant whilst travelling and having the baby whilst on the road (no, not literally!).

In nearly all cases, people have found the treatment and care to be just as good or superior to anything they would have received at home, and for a fraction of the cost. If you live in a country that supplies free healthcare for all of your needs, then this will not apply to you, but many countries do not operate that kind of service and it's usually far cheaper for their citizens to travel abroad to receive the treatment they need.

For example, a quick Google search reveals the average cost of a total knee replacement in the U.S. is almost $50,000. In Bangkok, it maxes out at $17,000. A savings of $33,000 will keep you travelling for a very long time!

But, people generally fear the change and fear the fact

that they aren't in their home country, with home comforts or a support network. The truth is that the clinics you find in cities such as Bangkok are incredible and are staffed by world class doctors and nurses who go to great lengths to ensure your level of comfort and care would far surpass anything you would expect at home.

Travel Mishaps

"Audaces fortuna iuvat (Latin) - Fortune favors the bold."
- Virgil

Not every challenge you will face along your journey will come in the shape of a medical emergency. Even if you follow all our travel tips and, despite the best planning in the world, you will likely run into a few setbacks during your travels. Here's just one example from our personal experience....

I stood there looking at the guy in disbelief. I couldn't process what he just told us. I was in shock, embarrassed, anxious and searching my mind for how this all could have gone so wrong. Clair looked at me for some kind of explanation, the kids stood rooted to the spot, heads upturned waiting for an answer with a worried look on their faces.

"What a fuck up." Those were my exact words.

I unloaded the bags back off the bus where I had just loaded them. This was the wrong bus. This bus was headed south from Seattle to Portland, not north across the Canadian border into Vancouver.

No, that bus had left half an hour earlier. Somehow, I had misread the ticket and after 15 months of solid travel, we had just missed our first bus, plane, train or automobile. It was sickening. It had to happen at some point, I guess, but it was still a huge kick in the nuts.

A four-hour bus journey from the centre of Seattle to Vancouver had seemed too easy. Perhaps I had let my 'travel' guard down?

I couldn't fathom it. I was gutted.

Stranded on the side of the road with all our luggage

and nowhere to go, we needed a plan and quick. The kind staff member on duty who had just delivered the crippling news let us borrow his phone so that we could call the company to find out what time the next bus to Vancouver left. I thanked him profusely and begged with the lady in the call centre to guarantee us tickets on the next bus out of Seattle.

We were advised that the next bus left in two and a half hours and that their policy was this: "Your purchased tickets can be used to board the next bus if, of course, there is room on the bus. If you want to guarantee seats, you need to repurchase six new tickets now, which will cost over $100 USD."

Bugger.

I asked how many seats were available and was advised that there were still fourteen seats left. But, there was no telling whether or not somebody might come in online to purchase tickets last minute.

Our choice was simple. Wait it out and try our luck, or cough up the cash to re-buy the tickets we already had in our hands!

We chose to wait it out.

Being in Seattle, it was easy to find the nearest Starbucks to get Wi-Fi and Skype fired up. We needed to let our next home swap host know what had transpired as he was scheduled to pick us up from the station in Vancouver.

Then we peppered the bus company with calls every twenty minutes to check the status of how many seats were left. We got a different answer every time and it was all becoming less clear and more stressful with every minute that passed. One person had even advised the opposite information and told us that we wouldn't be able to board the bus on the same tickets at all!

The guy who had originally delivered the bad news assured me that he was going to make damned sure that we got on the bus if the seats were empty, on his head be it. Just another example of awesome humanity and kindness that we encountered throughout our journeys.

In the end, our luck held, but our nerves were in shreds. Thankfully we were able to board the next bus and finally got on our way to Canada, albeit three hours late!

Upon our arrival at the Vancouver train station, we were met by Peter, our home swap host. Peter had already insisted that we borrow his car for the duration of our swap. He helped us load up and kindly drove us to the nearest supermarket so that we could stock up on some provisions. He then set us directions in the Sat Nav to the ferry terminal to catch our boat across to Bowen Island and waved goodbye.

However, time had again slipped away and we missed the 6.40 p.m. boat we had aimed for, only to be told that the next boat left in two hours!

Aaaaaaaagggghhhhh what a day!

Thank goodness for long summer evenings and the ferry terminal being in a pretty cove. We purchased some fish and chips, chatted to some locals and headed to the park where we waited for the next ferry to arrive.

This is one of the few situations that occurred on our travels that caused us more stress than was needed. But here's the deal, things like this happen in regular life too. And it would have likely happened whether we had kids travelling with us or not — they were not to blame, nor are they ever a reason to not travel!

A Dangerous World

One of the bigger excuses I hear for not travelling, however, would appear to be a little more serious than a missed bus. Concerned folks back home and strangers we meet along the way often ask, "With all the terrorism in the world at the moment, isn't it too dangerous to travel?"

To be honest, this question is met with a little disbelief on our part. It's amazing how the media is turning us all into mindlessly scared and hateful people.

The answer is, of course, NO! No, it is not too dangerous to travel and, no, we have not ever felt threatened and have yet to be disturbed by anyone or any event. Maybe we are lucky to not have been affected, but your chances of falling prey to terrorism isn't down to travelling. Perhaps even by travelling to many different places each month you are actually safer than commuting into the same 'targeted' city every day. Had you ever thought of that? Unfortunately, the news casters pick and choose events that will seem to be the most horrific and oftentimes twist the stories and use the same one or two pictures over and over again and label as many events as 'terrorist attacks' as possible. Now, obviously, it would be prudent to not travel through countries in the midst of troubles, be that civil wars, famines, droughts, natural disaster zones, etc., but don't discount countries just because of one off event that has recently happened there.

Have you ever considered the USA a dangerous place to travel? Nicholas Kristof of the New York Times famously wrote an article named, "More Americans have died from guns in the United States since 1968 than on battlefields of all the wars in American history."

Gun crime aside, the country also suffers from natural disasters such as deadly hurricanes, blizzards, cyclones, tornadoes, earthquakes, wildfires, droughts and floods. There are poisonous animals such as snakes, spiders and scorpions, there are alligators, sharks, bears and wild cats. The list goes on. They pretty much have it all!

Sobering thoughts indeed, yet somehow, we collectively never deem America an 'unsafe' country to visit. Please don't think for one second that I am 'hatin' on the old U.S. of A. No, not at all.

We spent almost two months there and travelled through Seattle, Tahoe, New York and Virginia and had an amazing time! I just want to highlight that prejudicing countries as dangerous and not fit to travel is wrong and will veer you away from the most incredible experiences.

So, turn yourself off from the noise and make good judgements founded on your own research and validation!

Don't Let Fear Decide

"**Frankly I didn't let myself get carried away trying to memorise every cockeyed thing, because the big thing in life, not only making the jump into Normandy, is that you have got to be able to think on your feet.**"
– Major Richard 'Dick' Winters

Too often, we bow to our fears when we are making big decisions. If you are on the verge of a long-term travel decision yourselves, then I am sure your mind is running wild with all kinds of awful situations you might find yourselves in. Lost in a foreign country, losing a passport, missing a plane, an accident, pickpockets, terrorist attacks and so on.

Once you let the fears take over and brainwash you, it's so easy to then push your dreams aside and carry on regardless in the 'cosy' life you feel you have created for yourself.

But, here's the thing, bad things will still happen to us in that 'cosy' life anyway, so what the hell are we really afraid of? A surprise pregnancy (been there) a demotion (been there), a hospitalisation of a family member due to some random health problem or freak accident (been there), car accident, sporting accident, fire, flood, blah blah blah, the list goes on, doesn't it?

Yes, we faced some challenges on our travels, shit happened and we dealt with it – just like you or anybody else in the world would have done. It's time to park our fears people and get on with it. The world is too big and too amazing to let our fears keep us from exploring it all!

The Homecoming

Easy, right? Wrong.

Reintegration is another hotly discussed topic among the long-term family travel groups. You will likely be thinking that coming home after an extended trip is easy, you just walk straight back in, everything is normal and as you remember.

Well yes, it is, but that is precisely the problem people face! Many returning families find coming 'home' to be a hugely difficult transition.

The first few weeks are great, lots of friends and family are overjoyed to see you and you enjoy catching up with everybody, having that feeling of homely comfort. But, gradually, over a few weeks you start to feel stifled and bound by the overwhelming sense of returning to the norm. Within a very short period of time, you find yourself slowly slipping back into being completely governed by the systems that you worked so hard to escape!

The main problem at work here is the fact that the returning families would have changed dramatically and are not the same people they were as when they left. You view things differently and have a totally different mindset towards situations. Your friends and family can't understand and you will almost certainly drift away from people with whom you were once very close and find it hard to reconnect.

Many people find it difficult to come home and make new friends and can end up feeling rather lonely, even though they are 'home.' I often see people discussing this topic on forums and have seen it on a professional level too. Far too often, I have seen expats relocated back to their old jobs in their home countries only to find that it's really unbearable for them to just slot straight back in as if nothing has ever happened.

For us, the concept of home has completely changed. We don't feel anchored to any country now. As much as we are English and call ourselves English, so many things have changed since we left the country in 1999. Most of that change has been personal development and we now see ourselves as global citizens rather than people who feel we should tie ourselves to one piece of land because we just so happened to be born there. Visiting England is a thrill for us now. We get to visit family and look at the country through the eyes of a tourist, which is a much better feeling to have than one of just simply returning.

In fact, this will always be the case now for our kids who were all born in Singapore, but never had citizenship there. If anybody asks them, 'where are you from', they struggle to answer. Some people look fondly at the youngest two and think it's cute that they don't know where they come from. 'Where do you live.' They press on, only to be met with 'Er, we kind of don't live anywhere. We travel the world.'

Quizzical looks then get shot our way and we have to start filling in the information.

As global citizens, we are always 'home'. It is impossible for me to fully advise anybody on the subject of reintegration since we have not traditionally done so and do not intend to. However, I did reach out to a few people who have gone through the process to get more insight on the topic. So, whilst I cannot provide my personal perspective, I can gift you the wisdom of others' experience.

I thank each contributor for their input and hope their insights bring you some needed guidance. Below are some of the responses to my questions.

Question – With the benefit of hindsight, what would you have done differently and what steps or preparation do you suggest others take?

"Don't return to the 'home place'. No matter what. Just don't go back. It's worse than you think it might be."
Micha Lunt Hooper.

Pretty strong advice from Micha, but this is exactly how she and her family felt after returning home, read on for more thoughts.

"We made the mistake of going back to the same everything: house, jobs, school. Kids were fine and happy to be back with friends. Husband and I were not. We were different people trying to fit back into our old lives. We had changed and it didn't fit anymore. I was depressed and despondent for months."
Rebecca Richler – www.Vanamos.net

Please note, I am not picking just the negative experiences here. I polled the travel forums and these were the most common answers I received.

As I stated before, this is a very hot topic and it stirs up a hidden emotion you have probably not considered, or even worse, dismiss. I thank Rebecca for being so open and frank about her feelings because it's so important to help people understand.

"We have just returned two months ago, so I feel I am not yet ready to completely understand it. But, a few points – my kids really wanted to go back, so for them it is easier than for me. Also, I knew I could not go back exactly to the same mental spot and welcomed changes. I wrote many

poems during our trip (in Hebrew, maybe they will be translated in the future) and decided to publish a book. I decided I want to sing more professionally and this is my goal for the coming year or two. I would recommend for re-integrators it is important to set new personal goals, to fulfill more personal dreams, not just traveling. Some things in life do benefit from living in one spot- find these, cherish and nourish them."
Shuli Hasheli.

Shuli offers great advice here, they had broken away and were used to pushing boundaries and barriers the whole trip. Once you have left the comfort zone it is so hard to go back to it. By setting herself new goals and projects she was setting her mind up to be active and engaged in new exciting experiences.

"We have been home two years and, while I won't say we are miserable, our trip changed us so much. We made the big mistake when we returned of jumping back into our old life the first year – that was a disaster. We were all too busy, too frenetic, and didn't feel like the tight family unit of our travels. Year Two was different. We slowed down. We said no to a LOT. We took small trips. We started treating our hometown differently, exploring, and planned our next trip. We just took a three-week road trip around the U.S. and it helped us figure out that we need to find the balance. The balance between our extreme world traveling and extreme home life. That is what we decided we will seek – balance. We now truly realize that no matter where you go, there you are. Sounds a bit trite writing that, but we realize now our family is very, very different than who we used to be after our travels and we like that family and need to work hard to maintain that."
Samantha Sackin.

Wow, nothing to add, incredible advice from Samantha.

Alisa and her family are an example of a family who found coming home to be a great experience. She is currently exploring this subject deeper and trying to find out what makes people successful or not in their homecoming, she shared with me in detail what worked best for them.

"Our family found reintegration quite easy. We were one of

those types who had said, 'We will never live in the U.S. again.' However, after living as expats for several years abroad, then traveling full-time for a year, we found ourselves on the fast-track to determining that a home abroad didn't check all the boxes on our wish list. We finally began to appreciate what our home country had to offer, and because of that we began anticipating the return.

Instead of returning to a home we had lived in before, we picked an entirely new place off the map (based on our list...the climate, outdoor recreation, community support, etc.). We were optimistically set on this one location, and admitted that if this didn't turn out to be "the" place, we were in trouble. Why? Because we'd literally crossed every other place off the list for one reason or another.

Fortunately, we'd been self-employed for over eight years when we returned, so there was no job that we had to plug ourselves into—and thus, no transition in that department. We'd been living a life of change since we married ten years previously, always moving every five to six months, so when we said, "We're buying a house and living here FOREVER", we made everyone's jaws drop to the floor.

We went in feet forward and eyes wide open. We accept that it isn't absolutely perfect---but no place in the entire world is. Instead, we embrace it all—flaws included---just as we had once embraced each and every foreign country that we encountered. If we can have the same open-minded nature about our own home country and the people living in it as we did when we were traveling, then we find we have much more compassion and understanding towards both our home culture and the people within it who are going about their daily lives in the only way they know how.

We've kept in touch with "our tribe" of traveling buddies abroad (always opening doors to friends traveling through), and meanwhile have built new bonds with many who have never even obtained a passport. We've immersed ourselves in our home community and have looked for ways to be impactful---serving & volunteering being some of the best tools we've found to teach us to love others and form new friendships."
Alisa – http://livingoutsideofthebox.com/

Incredible advice from Alisa. This is a topic she presents on at travel summits. The biggest take-away for me in that passage is the fact that nowhere in the world is perfect. We have, in the past, fallen into the trap of discussing and trying to figure out the exact best place in the world to live. We are now of the same mindset as Alisa: there isn't one, nor is there ever the perfect house, or the perfect car, or the perfect life. There will always be something slightly wrong, or you will always want something extra. As Alisa describes, it's key to embrace the flaws and recognise them for what they are, understand them and accept them.

Finally, World Schooling author (and my editor), Ashley Dymock de Tello was in the middle of her own reintegration process when she began editing this very section. She found these suggestions so useful in her family's decisions about how and where to settle down that I invited her to share her experience as a final insight into the complexities of reintegration.

To say I was apprehensive about moving back to the United States would be an understatement; but when my Mexican-born husband told me it was his turn to live in a different country and culture, I felt it would be hypocritical to deny him the opportunity. I was still dragging my heels, however, when an illness in the family put our plans to move to the U.S. on the fast track and we kicked it into high gear to get my husband's residency, sell all our belongings, and move from Mexico to be near my family.

Once we arrived, there were a number of important decisions to make in a very short period of time. My family was blown away at how quickly we were able to make each one. Our confidence in every choice was due to a significant amount of research before we had moved and the timely reading of this book.

While my work is location independent, my husband's profession is not and we decided that we would wait to see what his work options were before choosing where to settle down. We had set up a number of interviews before we arrived, several of which were located in the area where I grew up. I love my small hometown, but I knew the moment that we drove down those beautiful old country lanes that it wasn't the right place for us.

I was confused. How could I not want to live in a place that I loved so much?

That is when I came upon the jackpot of advice above. As so many of the other families had experienced, my travels had changed me. I was a different person and I needed a space where I could still be that new person, without expectations for any past version of myself.

With that knowledge, we chose to accept a job offer in a completely different city and settled down in a place where I never would have considered living eight years earlier when I left the United States to go travel the world.

We couldn't be happier with the decision. We are close enough to family and all my old childhood stomping grounds to share that part of my life with my husband and son, but we are also in a place that is completely new to both of us, allowing us to continue to grow and experience new things together. We get to go new places, create new friendships, and face new challenges every day, together.

In the short time since reintegration, I have also discovered that the world schooling mindset is something I didn't have to leave in Mexico. I have thoroughly enjoyed rediscovering my old home. Not only have things changed since I left but I am also more capable of seeing what was there all along. My travels helped me see just how much there is to learn from and give back to the world, even if that world is only on the other side of my doorstep.

- Ashley – www.BorderlessBooks.org

− − − − − − − − − − − −

Every family's situation is different. You might be able to fit straight back into your old lives and be just as happy as you were before, during, and after your travels. However, it is important to prepare and arm yourself with the knowledge that things might not go so well, and to keep an eye on how other members of the family are feeling and coping with it too.

Be prepared, and get some projects in place for when you arrive home!

− − − − − − − − − − − −

Thoughts From Clair

I sit here in Thailand in the summer holidays of 2017, reflecting on our last three years of travelling and being together as a family. I have loved every part of it. I have always loved travel and learning about other countries' history and culture, so of course I would jump at the chance to travel to so many places.

Add to that the privilege of being with my family day in and day out for the past few years and it's no wonder this has been amazing. Can you imagine the regret we would have felt if we had decided that we shouldn't have chosen this life?

More recently, whilst we haven't reintegrated back into our old life, we have chosen to settle down for a time in France. Our eldest daughter is now twelve years old and we have taken the decision to sit still for a little while so we can learn another language. Plus, the kids had expressed an interest in attending a school again. Kaitlyn, a pre-teen, is now looking to hang out more and more with her newly-made friends, which is inevitable for a girl of her age, and it will eventually happen to our other children.

I'm glad that we spent so much time with them exactly when we did, learning about their personalities, the way that they learn and what difficulties they have. For me, I also want to stay in the same place for a while and rediscover a sense of community. I feel the need to nest and have our creature comforts around us, although I'm also very much aware that we don't want to end up with as much stuff as we had before!

-- -- -- -- -- -- -- --

TOOLS AND TRICKS

If you would like to read further anecdotes from our travels, please visit the blog www.princesoffthegrid.weebly.com and click on the "One Year of Travel' story on the right-hand side of the
home page.

Find Alisa at http://livingoutsideofthebox.com/
Find Rebecca at www.Vanamos.net
Find Ashley at BorderlessBooks.org

Chapter 10
Life and Travel Hacks

"The best way to find out if you can trust somebody is to trust them."
- Ernest Hemingway

The sun had just set and the balmy heat of the day was gently being blown away by a wonderfully welcome breeze. I snapped open a can of Tiger beer and passed it across to my neighbour Jason, who gratefully took a deep swig of Singapore's national pride of lagers. He had just come home from a week flying long haul on the job for his current employers. As a pilot of fifteen-twenty years, Jason had seen the huge changes in the aviation industry and I always plugged him for great stories from yesteryear.

These were to be our final beers before we left for our travels, so we wasted no time getting straight into the legendary banter of tearing strips off each other in a way that only Australian and English men can understand and enjoy. Then, out of the blue, he told me a story from a flight he had just recently piloted. Something had shocked and really touched him, but also saddened him at the same time.

Happy to be returning home to his family, and with another drama-free flight under his belt, he pulled the plane to a halt outside the terminal and prepared for the post flight checks and paperwork. A knock at the door diverted his attention, and the lead stewardess appeared and passed him a note.

"I was asked to give this to you," she said with a huge smile on her face.

He took a piece of folded paper from her and looked

at the writing on the front.

"To the Pilot."

Unfolding the note, he was surprised to find a drawing of an airplane showing the pilot at the front flying through the blue sky with the sun in the air and mountains beneath.

Written below the picture was the message, "Thank you for flying us today and keeping us safe, Love Lucy 8."

His emotions ran rampant. He hadn't seen a note like this in over a decade. When he had first entered the business, this was a common sight, but slowly the notes and the whole excitement of air travel had disappeared from his life. To see a note like this again brought back all the feelings and emotions of pride and joy that he used to get after completing flights. It also made him sad that all of those emotions had pretty much disappeared over the decades.

I listened intently and took another swig of my beer, then most likely made some comment about him being a pansy. I mean he is an Aussie after all. But, secretly it did get me thinking deeper about what he said.

It seems that we now collectively view air travel as if it's our God-given right and widely regard the pilot as a glorified taxi driver. We don't take the time to ponder that there really are only a handful of people in the world that can competently and professionally fly these amazing machines. Plus, we are certainly collectively undervaluing the huge breakthroughs in technology and the freedom flying can bring us.

Look at it from this angle, in approximately just fifteen hours you can be on the other side of the world. Think about that for a second, it's mind boggling. Imagine telling that to somebody 100 years ago, they would never have believed you.

What's more, if you pick the right flights on the right days, you could well find yourself on the other side of the world in less than a day, and for less than a thousand pounds or dollars! So, next time you are having a bad day and want to make a change, bear in mind that by tomorrow you could be on the other side of the planet with a totally new perspective on life.

Inspired by my friend's story about his picture, we decided to get the kids to draw pictures for many of the pilots, and stewardesses, whenever we took flights. The results were astounding. The smiles and attention we got from the happy attendants was amazing. They fell over themselves to come and meet the kids and say thank you and pass them toys or free snacks.

On three occasions, we were even asked to stay on the plane after landing so that they could take us to personally meet the pilot and co-pilot in the cockpit. The pilots were all thrilled to meet the four children who had taken the time to draw pictures for them. They got to sit on the pilots' laps, wear their hats and learn about all the levers and buttons. On one flight, the co-pilot was female and she inspired our eldest two daughters to totally open their minds. They were so proud to see a lady at the helm and flying planes in what is assumed to be a very male-dominated and stereotyped profession.

This proves, again, that if you just take the time to think about and thank another person for their efforts, you really can break down some huge barriers between societies.

Whilst a simple example, little suggestions like this story from my pilot friend have made an enormous difference in our travel experiences. For that reason, this chapter is dedicated to some of the life/travel hacks we have leveraged over the last few years to enhance our travel and lives to the max. Of course, this is not a definitive guide and I would be ecstatic if you were to add your own hacks into the comments of our accompanying blog at princesoffthegrid.weebly.com/hacks. We are always keen to learn new ways to live life to the fullest and welcome any input at all.

Car Hire Hack

The travel hacks don't end with airplanes though! There are also some great hacks you can implement to get great deals on car rentals.

For example, the reason you found that super cheap deal on a car rental booking website is because the rental company has block-sold these car bookings at a very cheap rate to the booking engines so as to guarantee them a minimum amount of monthly earnings.

BUT, once you get to the desk to collect your car, the sales staff behind the desk are highly trained to upsell you so that they can make some real money out of you!

It is very easy for them to do this because you are an easy target. Quite simply, you are AFRAID. Selling to fear is easy, and a sales person with just the slightest of skill can be extremely good at helping you spend your money.

Think about it, you are now totally out of your comfort zone. You have landed in a foreign country, you might not be able to speak the language, you aren't used to driving on the other side of the car, the other side of the road, or using a different transmission. You fear getting lost or stopped by the police, you fear crashing, or getting your car stolen. You fear the habits of the local drivers and you fear fast motorways. You fear toll systems and strange traffic rules, you fear being beeped at for driving down the wrong side of the road.

You are tired from the journey and just want your damn car, so you just say yes, yes, yes to everything they suggest to get moving. Before you know it, the cheap car you rented is actually now three times more expensive than what you had budgeted!

After hiring countless cars over the last three years, here are my tips for getting that car at the exact rate you paid for it, because it is your right to. You have already paid, you have already entered into the contract and you don't want anything else on top.

CHECK at the point of booking the actual location of the rental agency. Sometimes you have to take a free train or shuttle bus to an offsite location to collect your car, which saves in money, but not in time, so choose your poison!

NEVER go to the desk as a full family, this is suicide. I always go alone or, at most, with my eldest daughter whilst my wife and other kids chill out on a bench a few hundred metres away.

If you all go to the desk together, the staff will start playing on your fears about child safety, there being too much luggage and your comfort being compromised. They will try to upsell you a larger, 'safer', more comfortable car and will likely tell you it's illegal to not hire child seats from them, at a ridiculous rate.

(If you want a clearer picture of child safety in car seats, make sure you watch Steven Levitt's Ted talk on the subject. It will open your eyes!)

They will then move on to other upsells listed below, I have included answers that you can use to overcome their tricks!

You only have the basic insurance, which doesn't cover you for much at all, you will need to take out our extra safe cover.

Refuse. We travel the whole time refusing the 'extra safe cover'. Our car hire insurance, like many, was automatically covered by the credit card we used to book the car.

There is also basic cover written into our general travel insurance, so we are legally covered and more than comfortable with the companies we have chosen to insure us.

Make sure you take a quick check of your policies and then just stand firm in the face of their attempts. It's actually quite fun to watch them slowly unravel as you overcome every one of their tricks.

It's not needed thank you, I already checked with my credit card company, which has included car insurance at the point of booking and I am also covered by my personal travel insurance, so I am fully covered.

At this point they will try to overcome your objection and counter you with, **"Are you sure the travel insurance properly covers you? In our experience, they only cover minor damage and flat tyres, but our cover is complete and just X amount per day. In the event of an accident, you will have no liability, there will be no extra charges to you."**

Listen to their objection carefully, and then reply. "I understand, but I literally called both companies two days ago and I know I am fully covered. I have used them for many years and am comfortable with their level of cover, but thank you for checking."

Would you like to have Sat Nav in the car? "No, thank you. We bought our own for this trip" or, "No, thank you. We have it on our phone."

Even if you don't have it, maps are a lot cheaper than

the rate for which they are going to loan you some crappy old Sat Nav!

You have limited miles only on this booking, you will be charged X amount per miles that you drive over that number, would you like to upgrade to unlimited miles?

Limited miles can mean anything up to 600 kms — which is a hell of a lot of driving, depending on where you are, of course. In our experience, we have never driven more than the limited miles allotted. But I would imagine that if you were halfway through your trip and you needed to upgrade to the unlimited mile plan it would take one phone call to the car rental agency to upgrade, So don't buy it before you need it!

"No, thank you, we won't be doing too much driving really, it's a holiday after all!"

For your convenience, you can return the car with low fuel, this will save you the hassle of finding a petrol station upon your return. We can fill the car ourselves, we get a much better rate than the gas stations, sometimes 30% cheaper.

No-brainer, right? Wrong.

If you agree to this, they will ask you to sign the paper saying you agree to return the car at low fuel and will charge you there and then for a full tank of gas.

The trick is this, they know that you will likely return the car with at least a quarter tank, in some cases even half full, but they have already charged you for a full tank so they make their margin on the difference. They will never refund you any gas you didn't use.

It's a ruse and one to be avoided. Always opt to return the car with the **same amount** of fuel with which you received it.

"No, thank you. We will just return it full, if the tank is full in the first place of course."

"But we have cheaper rates than the garages, you will be spending much more and saving with us."

"I understand, but that's fine. I would just like to return it as I found it, thank you."

"Oh, we have a brand-new car that has just come available today, it is a (premium name) that has only 450

kms on it. We can offer you this car at an extra special rate of just a further $8 U.S. per day. Would you like the (premium name)?

Oh, the shame! Now they are tugging at your material instincts! Don't be so shallow. "No, thanks. This car will be fine, thank you, I am no poseur!"

Hopefully, by now most of the upsells are over and you can start signing forms. All that is left to do is check over the vehicle with the attendant in the garage and note what scrapes and bumps are already there and off you go.

On rare occasions, we have been lucky and have been given a free upgrade to a bigger car with Sat Nav, so not all companies are bad. Just remember to have your wits about you and to enjoy the game. The more you say no, the quicker you might get your car because, unfortunately, the salesperson knows that there are fifty suckers in line behind you that will say yes, so it's better for them to move on.

Once you have your car and you have reached your destination, take some time to familiarise yourself with its workings. Cruise control can be a life saver for long journeys, make sure you know how to operate it. You can also change the language of all cars just by going through to the settings menu on the main console. We always change our language setting to English so we can understand any warnings that might light up.

Some modern cars have what's called 'Eco Drive', which you can activate at the push of a button. This will put the car into a different mode and will save you loads in fuel money, although you won't beat anyone off the lights!

Always have your cash, debit or credit card placed in an easy to reach location for any toll booths.

If you can activate a speeding alert, do it! Getting fines sucks, it costs you money and a huge amount of time and hassle and it is very easy to accidentally speed in an unusual car, especially on wide open roads.

— — — — — — — — — — —

TOOLS AND TRICKS

A video by yours truly showing a small hack for your car and overcoming 'filling up anxiety.' https://youtu.be/x91sQ5l4kpQ

Remember, wherever you are heading, always do a quick Google search for sharing economy companies that might be operating in that country. I previously highlighted how we found www.carnextdoor.com in Australia. There will be many copycat companies all over the world!

We have used rental car booking engines such as www.kayak.com or have used the Easy Jet or Ryanair car hire service after booking flights, as this will usually give you a much better discount too.

We have also used www.autoslash.com which automatically books, cancels and rebooks the cheapest deals for you through their website algorithm.

There are hundreds of sites out there and they are changing all the time. It would be futile listing them all here, a quick Google search will give you exactly what you need.

https://www.ted.com/talks/steven_levitt_on_child_carseats Interesting Ted Talk by Steven Levitt regarding child seats.

Flying Hacks

One of the keys to successfully hacking the airline system is to use Virtual Private Networks (VPNs). VPNs have been around for a long time now and most people have one or can get one at the click of the button.
For those of you uninitiated with the technology, a VPN basically masks your IP address, which hides your exact location. The interesting thing here is that if you are searching for flights or car hire, the prices can differ greatly from country to country. We have even found in some cases that switching

from Safari to Google Chrome has thrown up different results. You can also play around with currencies, whereby you can book in one currency much lower than in another. And this would still be a gain back to you even after the credit card exchange rate.

Don't just assume that the price you see is the best price available. Always look for other ways to find a better deal.

Even if Skyscanner is showing a cheap flight, visit the actual airlines website FIRST and check with them. Call them and ask if they can better the online price. It also helps to check if it is cheaper for you to buy two single tickets rather than a return. Amazingly, it is often times cheaper!

Another trick is to then check the airlines app. Companies are so eager to push all business online now that they are tripping over each other to offer better deals. If they have recently launched a new app or a new feature, then chances are that you will find a better deal that way

Use the airline's app to pre-check in and download your boarding passes. Some budget airlines charge you fines for not coming with a boarding pass, so make sure you do this! It saves you tons of time at the airport and keeps you paperless and clutter free.

_ _ _ _ _ _ _ _ _ _ _ _

TOOLS AND TRICKS

I am by no way an expert on VPN's, but the guys at VPN mentor are! They were kind enough to let me reference their work and below you can find an in depth article on how to save money on flights by using a VPN.
https://www.vpnmentor.com/blog/how-to-save-money-on-flights-with-a-vpn/

Travel search websites (there are so many now!) so be sure to do further research if you can't find what you are looking for:
www.skyscanner.com
www.tripadvisor.com
www.kayak.com

www.autoslash.com
www.googleflights.com
www.agoda.com
www.momondo.com

Water Hack

Tired of buying endless bottles of water and hate the fact you're contributing to the plastic in our oceans? We were, so we decided to do something about it.

Rather than keep buying and throwing away plastic bottles, we kept two large bottles and just asked people if they would be kind enough to refill them when they were empty. Walk into any bar, restaurant, hotel, pub, diner, canteen or shop and simply ask if it would be possible for them to kindly refill your bottle with drinking water.

I have done this hundreds of times and NEVER, not once, been turned down – even on budget airlines, where the staff are trained to try and sell you food and drinks to make some extra profit from you. Just take your bottle to the back of the plane where the staff are chatting and ask

It has worked every time.

Twitter Hack

Twitter isn't just a way for you to follow pop stars, football players and other Z list celebrities. If you view it as a way to send a text to pretty much anybody in the world, then you will soon start seeing amazing results. We used Twitter many times throughout our travels to connect with individuals and companies alike.

When we were in San Francisco, I tweeted the company weebly.com to say thank you for their brilliant website, which we have used to create our own website. Within minutes, they had tweeted back to us to arrange a family office visit! They were so lovely and showed us around the whole office, showcasing all of their cool office perks and even a secret room!

I also Tweeted Tim Ferriss when we were in San Fran to see if he would be interested in meeting up. Unfortunately, he was travelling, but he did hook us up with his top three restaurant choices in the city, one of which served the tastiest Burritos!

Feeling cheeky whilst in Washington DC, we took a family picture outside the White House and tweeted it to Obama and Michelle asking them if they would like to home swap with us!

Sadly, no response to that one, but it highlights the fact that you can literally tweet anybody who has an account. It's basically the same as sending a text to the president. It's an incredible way to connect and you should certainly not be shy of approaching any of your heroes or mentors.

Always Tweet to say thank you to the airlines you are travelling with as you never know, you might just get that upgrade or little extra care when checking in. Tweet restaurants, hotels, attractions or any other services that you have used, visited or are about to visit. It just takes a second and you might be hugely surprised by the responses.

Creating lists in Twitter is absolutely key to drowning out the deafening noise. Once you have your list created of the people you actually do want to hear from, bookmark your Twitter page in the browser whilst you are viewing your list. Now, each time you hit the Twitter bookmark in your toolbar it will take you directly to the list rather than put you into the oncoming traffic of the feed filled with B/S.

The Swimming Pool Hack

During a week's home swap in Bangkok, we were faced with the problem of the condominium pool being closed due to refurbishments. Yeah, huge bummer I hear you cry, but believe me, after a day of exploring the City, Palaces and Temples, you definitely want a cool dip. And if the carrot has been dangled and then taken away, you really feel the pinch, especially when you can see at least fifteen swimming pools from your 34th floor apartment windows!

Rather than remain beaten and have our spirits

dampened, we got onto researching the nearest hotels and calling around asking if they would be kind enough to let us come in and use the pool if we were to have lunch or drinks at their pool bars, I even booked a table online at one of them. But we struck out pretty hard and were told they would only consider letting in outside guests if we were to pay 500 THB per person, which for our family would have totalled around 65 GBP!

Undeterred, we packed our swimmers in a small bag and hit the streets. The plan was simple, walk along the road and enter every hotel until we got a yes, and believe me, when you walk into a hotel lobby with kids you get a lot of attention, smiles and understanding.

Hotel reception and concierge staff are trained to welcome anybody and are very professional, so engaging with them is very easy.

"Sawadee Khrup" means hello in Thai and is very well received when a foreigner makes the effort to say this first whilst raising their hands to prayer position and slightly bowing your head.

"Excuse me for asking, but my family and I are staying nearby in a condominium which has closed its pool for refurbishments. Would it be possible for us to come into your hotel, sit at the pool bar, order some drinks and food and use the swimming pool for a few hours?"

Five failures later we were welcomed with open arms by the staff of a small hotel who were so happy to meet our family. We spent all afternoon relaxing by their pool, swimming and of course drinking a few beers and some cocktails.

It was the perfect situation, they got some much-needed business and customers into their hotel and we got to use the pool and enjoy some drinks, which they even offered to us on happy hour!

As an added bonus, on our return to the apartment I flipped open the laptop to check emails and found this little gem from the F&B Manager of one of the hotels that had just turned us away!

Dear Mr. Daniel,

Greetings from …

I have been informed that you have booked a table at Pool Bar and you have come at the Bar today at 1 p.m. I didn't have the chance to meet you as you were gone. I would like to apologise about the miscommunication and the fact that we are usually charged outside guests to use our Pool and didn't communicate on the Website.

For this reason, I would like to invite you in our rooftop bar (Open daily from 5 p.m. until 1 a.m.) and experienced our service. I will be happy to offer you a bottle of wine and food (one pizza and tapas) to share if you decide to come enjoy our bar.

I hope that the misunderstanding didn't damage the image of our hotel and look forward to meeting you in case that you are coming back in our property,

Thanks & best regards,

Yes, the wine and pizza was most appreciated as I am sure you can imagine!

You'll discover your own travel hacks along the way, but these are just a few to get you started!

CONCLUSION

Deep somewhere in the tropics, a thirty-something male sleeps soundly in a huge king-sized bed. The bedside clock radio glows 5:44 a.m., everything is quiet.

The red devil numbers click to 5:45 a.m., the man sits bolt upright, instantly alert with a mix of fear and anxiety in his eyes. The silence is deafening, there is no alarm, there is no hushed radio station piping dreadful music at him. Confused, he glances at the clock: 5:45 a.m., then at his wife who is sound asleep next to him.

What the hell?

Where is he, why is he here and why did he automatically wake up at 5:45 a.m.?

Nervously, he surveys his surroundings. The room is strange, yet homely. The atmosphere is different, but welcoming. The smell is foreign, yet wonderful. Then the faint sound of the rhythmic ocean suddenly penetrates his thoughts, bringing him to his senses.

He breathes a sigh of relief and calms his mind. There is no need to rise out of bed today at 5:45 a.m., nor tomorrow. There is no alarm, there is no nine-to-five, there is no commute, there is no same old shit as yesterday.

Instead, there is a life that he

created, one that works for him and his family and one that he has complete control over. And this new life can wait another few hours until he is ready to wake up and enjoy it.

Silently, he lays back onto the pillow and turns over to spoon his loved one, he falls back into a wonderful slumber and dreams about the endless opportunities the day ahead might bring to his family.

The End.

Acknowledgements

To my wife Clair and our four wonderful children Kaitlyn, Sophia, Lauren and Samuel. Thank you all for trusting in me. What I asked you to do was massive, huge, gargantuan! Leaving your friends and the country of Singapore that you all knew and loved as home was a huge decision. If it were not for your combined bravery and willingness to push yourselves out of your comfort zones then our amazing journey over the last three years (so far) would never have come to fruition.

Without your blessing, this grand act of 'delusion' would have been pushed into the draw of 'Dad's bad ideas' and forgotten forever. Together, we stood to face and explore the world as one unit and we won, every day.

To my parents, to whom, naturally, I owe my life. Without you, there would be no me, and I would not have had the opportunity to explore this planet as much as I have to date. Thank you for your support and help in all aspects of our lives, and long may this journey continue!

To the many friends and family that we have stayed with along the way, you have been so generous in helping us achieve our goal. When we needed help you were there with a roof and a bed, food, storage space for the things we decided to keep, love, caring advice and much more. You continue to help us with administrative issues such as banking, investments and health policies. Our support network has been fantastic and we can't thank you all enough, it would have been a lot harder to achieve without you.

To Tim Ferriss, many people have pointed out that this book, my book, featured too heavily around your own work, ideas and practices. I was told that I should not hide behind your success, or ride your coattails, use my own story as it stood on its own merits, not somebody else's. However, I would not be here today if it were not for your writing.

Imagine if you had bowed to self-doubt and had ducked out of writing *The 4-Hour Workweek*. Imagine if you had buckled under the pressures of criticism or rejection. Imagine if you had given into the masses and let them cut down the 'Tall Poppy.' Your work inspired me to find a better life, not just for me, but for my family and for the generations that will follow.

I can't thank you enough, and can never repay you, I hope these words go some way to crushing any self-doubts that linger over your future projects. Never stop writing, ever, it's too important to too many people.

To the other influencers in my life, many who have been featured in this book, or have been highlighted by their quotes, thank you. Please understand that your hard work is making a difference, never stop, keep pushing, the world needs your insights, big ideas and huge kicks up the butt!

To all the people who said, 'Hey Dan, you should write a book, it's amazing what you have achieved, people need to know how you did it and that this lifestyle is possible, there are millions of people who would love to do the same.' Thank you, I think. Writing this book has been a journey like no other, it has been a grind at times, but I have thoroughly enjoyed it, and I hope my writing has lived up to your expectations and belief in me.

I don't know if it was the tipping point of the 101st person suggesting I write a book, or if it was the fact that it was you @scottwoodward. Your own story is and always has been an inspiration for me and I hope that one day you find your own courage to face this task of putting fingers to keys and helping others follow the dream and goals you set yourself.

To my editor Ashley Dymock de Tello. Thank you for seeking me out and connecting with me, reading then re-reading my work, and listening to my opinions. Your own work on this subject was a shining light and deserves great accolades. We find ourselves at the pointy end of a paradigm shift and fundamental change in the basic concepts and experimental practices of education. It will be truly interesting to see how this goes on to play out on a global scale. I am proud to have stood shoulder to shoulder with you on this most important subject.

To anybody looking to explore the path of writing and publishing their own book, I fully recommend Ashley's service. She is a location independent world schooling mum and can be found through her publishing company www.BorderlessBooks.org, or you can contact her at info@borderlessbooks.org.

To Richard Harvell of Bergli Books at Schwabe. Thank you for your time and early advice in the infancy of this project, you were a great source of insight and inspired confidence in me to put fingers to keys!

To Debbie Wosskow and her brother Ben. Thank you so much for founding the website that changed our lives. If it were not for Love Home Swap we would never have travelled as far and as wide as we have. You changed our lives for the better, forever. Keep up the great work within the sharing economy, it's too important not to, you are changing 1000s of families lives for the better!

To all of the people we have home swapped with, thank you from the bottom of our hearts. Your generosity and willingness to share your homes, cars, knowledge, friends, family, hospitality and love has enabled us to create an incredible lifestyle and reinstall our faith in humanity!

To any haters, doubters, or soon to be trolls, whoever your negative people might be. Thank you for pushing me to prove you all wrong. If it weren't for you I wouldn't be living the life I now see as my own, and over which I have full control.

I sincerely hope you conquer your own demons one day and go on to live a long and happy life.

"I like to think that today is the best day of my life and tomorrow will be the next best day of my life. And if you think that way, you're living for the beauty of today."
- Conrad Anker

To www.99designs.com for creating such an awesome platform for people to connect with designers from all over the world. My book cover was designed by user Abdo_96, a gifted professional who has designed many other book covers.

To Guns and Roses and The Stone Roses, thank you for your music. I have no idea how many times I looped your albums over and over as I wrote this book. My favourite songs? "Welcome to The Jungle" and "I Wanna Be Adored"!

To you, the reader, thank you for making it through the book. Not in my wildest dreams did I ever think this would come to fruition. If you have made it this far, I hope every word has kept you interested and entertained. Above all, I hope it has opened up a few doors you never thought could possibly be opened.

Take action with something you learnt here in these pages, you won't regret it, and it will lead to much greater things, I promise you.

Lastly, stay inquisitive. Always look for the other route and don't fear stepping outside of your comfort zone, for it's out there that great things will and do occur.

Daniel Prince
Somewhere in the South West of France Dordogne Region
July 2017

For speaking engagements, interviews or events please contact me via the blog at www.princesoffthegrid.weebly.com

Or find me -
@princey1976 on the Twitter
Princes Off The Grid on Facebook

Bonus Life Lesson!

Having almost completed the book, and with everything in order, it was hard for me to figure out exactly where to drop this story into the flow of things. It happened as we were travelling through Thailand during the summer of 2017. I think it is an important story that needs to be heard, and thought deeply about, and I didn't want to sideline it.

Rather than simply jam the story somewhere in the book I decided to add it as an afterthought.

Life Through a Different Lens

We crossed the bridge and walked a few 100 meters along the track in the direction of Burma. Our tour guide stopped us and asked the sole man in a tiny guardhouse what time the train would be coming. He turned to us with a big smile and informed us, "Train come in five minutes, we very lucky, only come two times a day!"

With that news, we turned on our heels and walked briskly back down the railway towards the bridge where we could step onto the relative safety of some small viewing platforms just beside the track.

We were on the famous Bridge on The River Kwai, which had taken us a three-hour drive to reach from Bangkok. Our tour guide, now our good friend, Khun (The Thai equivalent of - Mr.) See was employed by our home swap host to look after his apartment and tend to his guests' needs whilst he was out of town.

Khun See had been an invaluable source of information and, for much reduced rates compared to other tour guides in Bangkok, had helped us around the city and taken us on this journey to the River Kwai via amazing temples, museums and graveyards of POW victims of the Thailand to Burma death railway.

The tracks began to rumble as the train pulled closer to the bridge, it then stopped as the driver made sure the track was completely clear and exchanged some words with the guard who was now waving him through. With the all-clear, the driver slowly pulled onto the bridge and started tiptoeing across.

From our viewing platform on the bridge, we could literally touch the train as it edged past us. The tourists travelling the notorious railway were hanging out of the window and waving at the onlookers. Naturally, we all waved and smiled back, taking pictures of the spectacle.

Out of one window I noticed a transgender male smiling and waving effeminately at the children. It struck me again how strange it was that there are so many transgender people in Thailand. What was it with this country that seemed to produce so many? Thailand is famously known for its ladyboys and has annual national competitions to judge and award the prettiest ones. The stakes are high and the prize money could certainly change the lives of the winners, along with the celebrity status too!

Was it a genetic disorder I wondered?

Seeing the same ladyboy Khun See caught his eye, pursed his lips a little and said 'Suwai' in a slightly feminine way. This resulted in a huge blush and embarrassed smile back at him as the transgender man slightly hid his face behind a fan he had been using to keep himself cool.

I turned to Khun See and asked him what Suwai meant, he told me it meant beautiful. I was stunned.

At first, I thought maybe he had been a little ungracious and had shown contempt or sarcasm towards the man, but I could see in his eyes this wasn't the case at all.

"Do they like it when people say that to them?"

"Yes of course, they very much like to be told this, they love it when another man says they look beautiful, did you see him smile?"

"Why are there so many? I asked.

"In Thailand nobody cares, we tell them they look beautiful, it makes them happy. Many ladyboy from other countries come here, from Singapore, Indonesia, China, Malaysia, India, many country, because they can be themselves here. They accepted, they don't have to hide."

Unbelievable, with that simple explanation Khun See had made me see the big picture. I felt ashamed that I had been shallow enough to think that there was some kind of genetic default at work, where really all that is happening is complete and total human acceptance.

Of course there aren't more transgender males in Thailand. In fact, there could likely be more transgender males per capita in many other countries, it's just that in their countries they are not allowed to be who they want to be. They have to hide and cover up their 'shame'. In Thailand they don't have to, they can be who they want, when they want, where they want and even be complemented on who they are on a daily basis!

Yet, in the western world we are still raging ridiculous arguments about the legality of same sex marriages. We see ourselves as so further advanced than other countries and cultures, but could it be we are actually still just stuck in the dark ages?

Open your ears and eyes, always be a keen questioner, engage with as many of the local people as you can and be prepared to learn far more than you thought possible!